THE LIBRARY ON DISPLAY

I

This volume was produced to accompany the public display
of the MS Med. Palat. 218–20 on the occasion of the European Heritage Days
("Le grandi strade della cultura: un valore per l'Europa"), 29–30 September 2007

Photographs
Biblioteca Medicea Laurenziana, Florence
By permission of the Ministero per i Beni e le Attività Culturali.
Unauthorized reproduction is strictly prohibited.

© 2007 Mandragora. All rights reserved.

Mandragora s.r.l.
Piazza del Duomo 9, 50122 Firenze
www.mandragora.it

English translation by
Jeremy Carden, Andrea Paoletti

Edited, designed and typeset by
Monica Fintoni, Andrea Paoletti, Paola Vannucchi

Printed in Italy

ISBN 978-88-7461-102-7

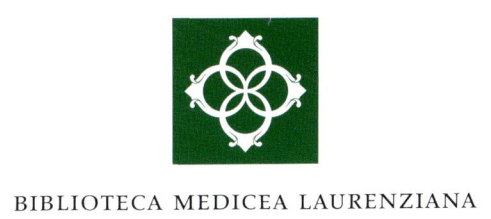

BIBLIOTECA MEDICEA LAURENZIANA

the world of the aztecs

IN THE FLORENTINE CODEX

Mandragora

PREFACE

Rare and valuable items, especially codices, are known in Italian as *cimeli*, from the Latin *cimelium* and the Greek *keimelion*. There are a great many of them in the Biblioteca Medicea Laurenziana, because the works that make up its collections have always been chosen for their antiquity, rarity and beauty.

However, even this traditional definition, generally used to describe valuable museum pieces, appears inappropriate and inadequate when applied to the partially autograph manuscript of the *Historia general de las cosas de Nueva España*, by the Spanish Franciscan friar Bernardino de Sahagún.

Despite being almost five hundred years old, this work could not be more topical or pertinent with regard to an issue that is now very much to the fore—the coexistence of different civilizations. In terms of the quality of the overall project, the impartiality with which the material was gathered and narrated, and the underlying purpose of the undertaking, inspired purely and simply by a desire for knowledge, the *Historia* testifies to the way in which Europe proved able, in the past, to learn about and describe other civilizations, and remains an example for the future about how Europe might fruitfully engage with diversity.

A simple Franciscan missionary—and the fact that he belonged to one of the most revolutionary orders in Church history is hardly a coincidence—, Bernardino was sent to Mexico to spread the true faith. While he was there he lovingly and systematically set about gathering accounts of a world that was dying out, in order to preserve this knowledge for future generations.

Bernardino doggedly pursued his task for some thirty years, heedless of the plague raging around him. He was assisted by a group of village elders who de-

scribed in their own language, Nahuatl, the flowers, fruits and animals of the natural environment, the habits and customs of a people with a complex set of traditions, and the rites of a strict religion that demanded human sacrifices to appease often hostile gods. When words failed to evoke habits, customs or popular beliefs, highly graphic illustrations not unlike the very best modern cartoons supplemented and enhanced a bilingual account that was utterly non-judgemental and without a trace of prejudice.

It is hardly surprising that this encyclopedia of the Meso-American civilization was not viewed with favour by King Philip II of Spain, and it is no accident that this magnificent version, which eventually found its way to Europe, should have ended up in the collection of the enlightened Medici dynasty; and that from there it should have passed many years later into the Biblioteca Medicea Laurenziana, where it took its rightful place alongside other illustrious expressions of universal culture.

This extraordinarily interesting codex, which formed the centrepiece of the large-scale *Aztecs* exhibition held consecutively in 2002 and 2003 at the Royal Academy of Arts in London and the Martin-Gropius-Bau in Berlin, is now being presented in Florence on the occasion of the European Heritage Days. The Florentine Codex appears particularly relevant to the theme of the event, "The Great Paths of Culture: A Value for Europe".

This publication, which also serves as the catalogue for the display of the manuscript, has been made possible thanks to the contribution of Ida Giovanna Rao, manuscript keeper of the Biblioteca Medicea Laurenziana, Diana Magaloni of the Instituto de Investigaciones Estéticas of the Universidad Nacional Autonóma de México, and the archaeologist Alessandra Pecci, who has specific expertise with regard to Meso-American civilization. Alessandra Pecci will also give a lecture in which she will comment on slides of the most significant amongst the 2,468 illustrations in the *Historia general de las cosas de Nueva España*.

I would like to thank Mario Curia and his editorial team at Mandragora for having made this publication possible. It is one of many initiatives aimed at making the treasures of the Biblioteca Medicea Laurenziana more widely known, in particular to the Italian public, which perhaps less than others has had occasion to appreciate its universal and enduring values.

Franca Arduini
Director, Biblioteca Medicea Laurenziana

THE FLORENTINE CODEX

Florence, Biblioteca Medicea Laurenziana, Mediceo Palatino 218–20
[Bernardino de Sahagún], [*Historia general de las cosas de Nueva España*]
1575–7; 318 × 210 mm
3 vols., fols. 353, 375, 495; paper; contemporary plateresque binding (Spain)
Provenance: Biblioteca Palatina Granducale, Florence; from 1783, Biblioteca Medicea Laurenziana, Florence.

Its original four volumes now bound in three, the codex contains the final version of the *Historia general de las cosas de Nueva España* ("General History of the Things of New Spain"), an encyclopedic work in twelve books by the Spanish Franciscan friar Bernardino de Sahagún (1499–1590), who arrived in Mexico as a missionary after the Spanish conquest of the region by Hernán Cortés (1519–21). The result of research work carried out between the late 1540s and 1569, the *Historia general* constitutes an extraordinary attempt at Christianization through cultural understanding rather than force. Books 1–3 of the work deal with the religious beliefs of the indigenous peoples (gods, myths, religious festivals, sacrifices, idolatry), 4–5 with astrology and divination; Book 6 includes a selection of prayers and formal speeches exemplifying various forms of Nahua rhetoric; Book 7 is about the Sun, the Moon and the stars; Book 8 is devoted to local history (rulers and nobles), Book 9 to commerce (merchants and craftsmen, including goldsmiths and featherwork artists), Book 10 to Aztec society (virtues and vices, illnesses and remedies); Book 11, the longest in the codex, is a treatise on natural history; Book 12 recounts the Spanish Conquest and the fall of Tenochtitlán.

Although the lower margin of fol. 328r in the first volume bears Sahagún's signature, the manuscript was written by various scribes in Tlatelolco between the end of 1575 and the beginning of 1577. On each page are two columns of text, one in Spanish, the other in Nahuatl, the language most widely spoken amongst the Toltecs, Chichimecs and Aztecs.

The Spanish translation had been carried out at the request of Rodrigo de Sequera, Commissary General of the Franciscan Order and a great admirer of the *Historia*; Sequera was thus implementing an order given by Juan de Ovando, President of the Council of the Indies, who was keen to discover more about this illustrated encyclopedia of Mexican civilization before the Conquest. Philip II, king of Spain from 1556 to 1598, was not in favour of this liberal approach to the conversion of the indigenous peoples, and sometime around 1577 ordered that all of Sahagún's writings and the material he had gathered for the *Historia* should be sent to Spain so as to prevent the work's circulation. Sequera managed to avoid handing over this codex, and presumably brought it to Europe in the first months of 1580.

In 1589 the Florentine artist Ludovico Buti (active 1560–1603) painted a ceiling fresco in the Uffizi that was obviously inspired by the illustrations in the manuscript, a clear indication that the codex had already entered the Biblioteca Medicea Palatina (either by purchase or private donation), where it complemented the wealth of Mexican objects in the non-European collections of the Medici grand dukes Francesco I (1574–87) and Ferdinando I (1587–1609). It lay in obscurity until 1793, when the head of the Biblioteca Medicea Laurenziana, Angelo Maria Bandini (1757–1803), described it in the final volume of his monumental *Catalogus* along with the other codices in the grand-ducal library that had been chosen for inclusion in the Laurentian Library by order of Peter Leopold of Habsburg-Lorraine, grand duke of Tuscany from 1765 to 1790.

Ida Giovanna Rao
Biblioteca Medicea Laurenziana

BIBLIOGRAPHY. *Bibliotheca Leopoldina Laurentiana seu Catalogus manuscriptorum qui nuper in Laurentianam translati sunt, sub auspiciis Ferdinandi III...*, Angelus Maria Bandinius ... recensuit, illustravit, edidit, Florentiae 1793, 454–6; Bernardino de Sahagún, *Historia general de las cosas de Nueva España. V. Códice Florentino*, edited by Francisco del Paso y Troncoso, Madrid 1905; Bernardino de Sahagún, *Florentine Codex. General History of the Things of New Spain*, translated from the Aztec into English, with notes and illustrations by Arthur J.O. Anderson and Charles E. Dibble, 13 vols. in 12, Santa Fe, N.M. 1950–82; Donald Robertson, *Mexican Manuscript Painting of the Early Colonial Period: the Metropolitan Schools*, New

Haven, Conn. 1959; Bernardino de Sahagún, *Códice florentino. Historia general de las cosas de Nueva España*, facsimile edition, 3 vols., Mexico City 1979; Pietro Corsi, "Il Codice Fiorentino: nota storica", *FMR*, 1 (1982), 80–3, 134–5; Bernardino de Sahagún, *Historia general de las cosas de Nueva España*, introducción, paleografía, glosario y notas de Alfredo López Austín y Josefina García Quintana, 2 vols., Madrid 1988; Enrico Spagnesi, "Bernardino de Sahagún, la natura in Messico, l'arte a Firenze", *Quaderni di Neotropica*, 1 (1993), 7–24; Ida Giovanna Rao, in *Aztecs*, exhibition catalogue (London, Royal Academy of Arts, 16 November 2002–11 April 2003), [exhibition curators Eduardo Matos Moctezuma and Felipe Solís Olguín], London 2002, n. 344, 487–8.

* * *

The *Historia general de las cosas de Nueva España* is a twelve-volume encyclopedic work about the people and culture of Central Mexico compiled by Fray Bernardino de Sahagún and a group of knowledgeable native assistants in the wake of the Conquest. The original manuscript is part of the collection of the Biblioteca Medicea Laurenziana in Florence (Mediceo Palatino 218–20) and is commonly referred to as the Florentine Codex.

The work had probably entered the Medici collections by 1588. According to a recent study, at that time Philip II of Spain was keen to strengthen diplomatic relations with Florence, and in 1588 sent Luis de Velasco as his ambassador to express condolences following the death of Grand Duke Francesco de' Medici (1587) and to congratulate his brother, Cardinal Ferdinando, for his ascension to the grand-ducal throne. Ferdinando was a keen collector of rare manuscripts and the Florentine Codex would have made a perfect gift.

In 1558 Sahagún, who had been conducting research into indigenous cultures since the 1540s, was asked by his superiors in the Franciscan Order to write an account of the religion and customs in New Spain that would help missionaries in their work to convert the indigenous people to Christianity. Fray Bernardino modelled the project along the lines of medieval encyclopedias and secured the assistance of two important groups of natives: the elders of a number of towns in Central Mexico (the *principales*) and some young members of the Nahua nobility who were being educated by the Franciscans at the College of Santa Cruz in Tlatelolco, Mexico City. The *principales* agreed to answer questionnaires prepared by Sahagún about their culture and religion, and their responses were recorded in their own pictorial form of writing. The young Nahua students interpreted the images and expanded the answers, phonetically transcribing Nahuatl—the language that was spoken in Cen-

tral Mexico before the arrival of the Europeans—using Latin letters (the so-called 'alphabetic' Nahuatl). These writings formed the basis of the final text. The students also illustrated the twelve books of the codex. Sahagún then reviewed the Nahuatl text and added his own Spanish translation. The whole process took almost thirty years and the work was finally completed in Tlatelolco in 1577.

The pages of the twelve books that comprise the Florentine Codex are arranged in two columns: on the right is the original Nahuatl text, on the left Sahagún's Spanish translation.

The 2,468 magnificent illustrations are for the most part in the left-hand column, where the text is shorter. An original and novel mode of expression, these illustrations are an adaptation of the ancient Nahua tradition of painting-writing, the images of which were visually compelling and held the status of 'sacred word'. The illustrations of the codex creatively combine the syntactic and symbolic traits of the ancient tradition with the principles and formal qualities of European Renaissance painting, representing a response to the new reality of Mexico in the aftermath of the Conquest.

On account of the codex's unique material features, a range of in-depth scientific tests were carried out on its illustrations as part of a research project conducted by the Instituto de Investigaciones Estéticas of the Universidad Nacional Autónoma de México (Mexico City), with the support of the Chemistry Department of the University of Florence and the Kunsthistorisches Institut in Florenz, and the collaboration of the Opificio delle Pietre Dure (Florence) and the Biblioteca Medicea Laurenziana.

The Florentine Codex was composed in dire circumstances. In the prologues to Books 1 and 2, Sahagún recounts that twenty years had elapsed from when he started collecting information to when the Nahua students finished a first draft in alphabetic Nahuatl in 1569. The following year, 1570, Sahagún handed over the work to his superiors for inspection. Some of them expressed appreciation, but it was objected that employing scribes was a waste of money and that he should continue on his own. But Sahagún was over seventy years old at the time and his trembling hands could barely hold a pen. To compound matters further, it soon began to be suggested that works of this kind might encourage idolatry.

Fortunately for the fate of the work the situation changed when a great humanist, Fray Rodrigo de Sequera, was appointed Commissary General of the Franciscan Order in 1575. In the meantime Sahagún had succeeded in recovering the original manuscripts, which had been scattered throughout the province; Sequera asked

de la fiesta   Tecuilhuitontli. fo. 46.

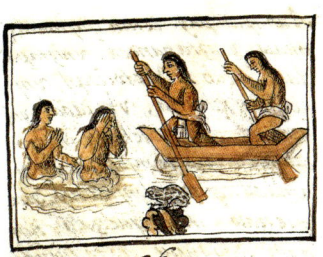
26.

¶ Capitulo ~~octauo~~, de la fiesta y cerimonjas, que se hazian enlas kalendas, del septimo mes, que se nombraua. Tecuilhuitontli.

ynieiuhquj mec viloatz, mec tla qujqujxtilo, tlaceoalo intolpepechtli, in vncan calmecac: tlaquj qujxtilo, calteputzco contlatlaca. Je izequjch, vncan tlamj y, yn ilhujtl, in etzalqualiztli.

¶ Injc ~~cep~~ ouA onchiquaçe capitulo. Vncan moteneoa ynjlhuitl, yoan intlamauiztililiztli, in muchioaia, ynipan vel ic ce milhujtl, ie chicome metztli, in mjtoaia: Tecuilhuitontli.

Al septimo mes, llamauan teujlhujtontli: eneste mes, hazian fiesta, y sacrificios, ala diosa de la sal, que llamauan Vixtociuatl, era la diosa, de los que hazen sal. Dezian que era hermana, delos dioses de la pluuja, y por cierta desgracia, que vuo entre ellos, y ella la persiguieron, y desterraron alas aguas saladas, y alli inuento la sal, de la manera que agora se haze, contin ajas, y con amontonar la tierra salada: y por esta inuencion, la honrrauan, y adorauan los que tratan en sal. los atauios desta diosa, eran de color amarilla, y vna mjtra, con muchos plumajes verdes, que salian della, como penachos alto, que del ayre

Tecuilhuitontli: ynin qujcaia, in muchioaia, inte cuilhuitontli, no cempoalilhujtica: auh vnâ mjquja, vncan te qujuh vetia vncan teumjquja in vixtocioatl, ynjnteouh iztatlaca, iztachiuhque. Jnjn vixtocioatl, iuh mjtoa qujlmach in veltiuh catca intlaloque: yoan qujlmach yiçoftioan in tlaloque: contlama Hi ic qujnqualanj, ic qujnio lltlaco, inca mocaiauh, ynj oqujchtoan: auh njman ic qujto~~toc~~aque ynjn veltiuh vmpa ynjztapan: vmpa qujnextito ynjztatl, ynjuh ioli, ynjuh tlacati, ynjuh muchioa iztacomjtl, yoan iztaxalli

Fray Bernardino to translate the work, providing everything that he and his team of Nahua scribes and painters needed in order to complete their task.

However, the scribes and painters of Tlatelolco were to face an even greater ordeal. In 1576 an epidemic killed 80 per cent of the indigenous population of Mexico City. In spite of their suffering and the ever-present threat of contagion, the authors continued their work in the austere rooms of the College of Santa Cruz.

Sahagún himself describes their dreadful plight in the Spanish text of Book 11, which deals with the natural world, suddenly interrupting his translation to observe (220, fols. 389v–90r):

> In this year 1576, in the month of August, a great universal pestilence began. It has been three months now since it started and many have died and continue to die, more and more each day … I am now at Tlatelolco in Mexico City, and I see that since it started and until today, the 8th of November, the number of dead has continued to raise; from ten to twenty, from thirty to forty, from fifty to sixty and eighty, and I know not what will happen from now on. In this pestilence, as in the other I mentioned before, many have died of hunger and of thirst, and lack of care and assistance: because it often happened in the past and happens today that an entire household falls sick and there is no one even to bring a simple jar of water.

The making of the Florentine Codex is therefore surrounded by disease, grief and death. Some of the painters are known to have died in the epidemic and this experience made the survivors painfully aware that their people and culture were threatened by extinction. In spite of the tragic circumstances, however, the team of scribes and painters continued their work.

In view of all this, a number of important questions inevitably arise. What significance did this work hold for the men in Tlatelolco and for Fray Bernardino? What importance should we attribute to their experience and frame of mind in our assessment of their incredible achievement? In the midst of devastation, this group of painters and scribes worked to create twelve books where perfect harmony is achieved between the handwritten bilingual texts and the coloured drawings produced in different formats and sizes according to the subject matter of each chapter. The result, a truly unique masterpiece, is highly significant from many points of view: it is the most important source for the study of ancient Meso-American history; it is also a history of the conflict, negotiation and dialogue between two different worlds and cultures; most importantly, however, it is a carefully and skilfully crafted work of art whose material qualities and historic context bear the indelible marks of an epic battle for survival.

It is a privilege for us today to be able to admire and study this magnificent collective work produced in Tlatelolco by the Nahua elders and students and by Fray Bernardino de Sahagún in the course of one of the most fraught yet momentous periods of world history.

> Diana Magaloni
> *Instituto de Investigaciones Estéticas, UNAM*
> *Mexico City*

For a survey of the extensive literature dealing with the Florentine Codex and Bernardino de Sahagún, see Miguel León-Portilla, *Bernardino de Sahagún, first anthropologist*, translation by Mauricio J. Mixco, Norman, Okl. 2002 (original edition Mexico City 1999), 291–314, and *Sahagún at 500. Essays on the Quincentenary of the Birth of Fr. Bernardino de Sahagún*, edited by John Frederick Schwaller, Berkeley, Calif. 2003, 275–94.

IMAGES FROM THE CODEX

by ALESSANDRA PECCI

1. The gods

Florence, Biblioteca Medicea Laurenziana, Med. Palat. 218, fol. 10r

Following the traditional division of knowledge common to many European encyclopedic works, the Florentine Codex deals with "all things divine (or rather idolatrous), human and natural of New Spain". The first book is therefore devoted to superior beings, namely the gods worshipped by the Aztecs, and the second to the religious festivals with which they paid homage to them.

Sahagún describes the principal gods in the Aztec pantheon, succinctly listing their distinctive physical features, attire, main functions and the festivals dedicated to them. To make them more readily comprehensible to European readers, he sometimes likens them to figures from Graeco-Roman mythology: Huitzilopochtli ("Uitzilobuchtli" in the codex) is defined as "another Hercules" and Tezcatlipoca as "another Jupiter".

Huitzilopochtli (opposite, top left) was the patron god of the Aztecs, who guided them on their pilgrimage from Aztlán, the mythical 'white land' of their origins, to the 'promised land' where in 1325 they founded the city of Tenochtitlán (later Mexico City). Huitzilopochtli was the god of war—like Hercules he was huge, immensely strong and warlike—and to him was dedicated one of the two shrines of the Templo Mayor (the Great Pyramid) of Tenochtitlán.

The other shrine was dedicated to Tlaloc (opposite, bottom right), 'he who makes things sprout', the rain god, the life-giver, divine water, who lived on the highest mountains where clouds form. Tlaloc was associated with the agricultural world, the fertility of the land and its economic implications. He was a benevolent deity because he provided the water that irrigated the land and enabled the growth of grass, trees, plants, fruit and everything necessary for sustenance; however, he also had a negative side to him, since he was responsible for the lightning, frost, floods and hailstorms that destroy crops.

I. THE GODS

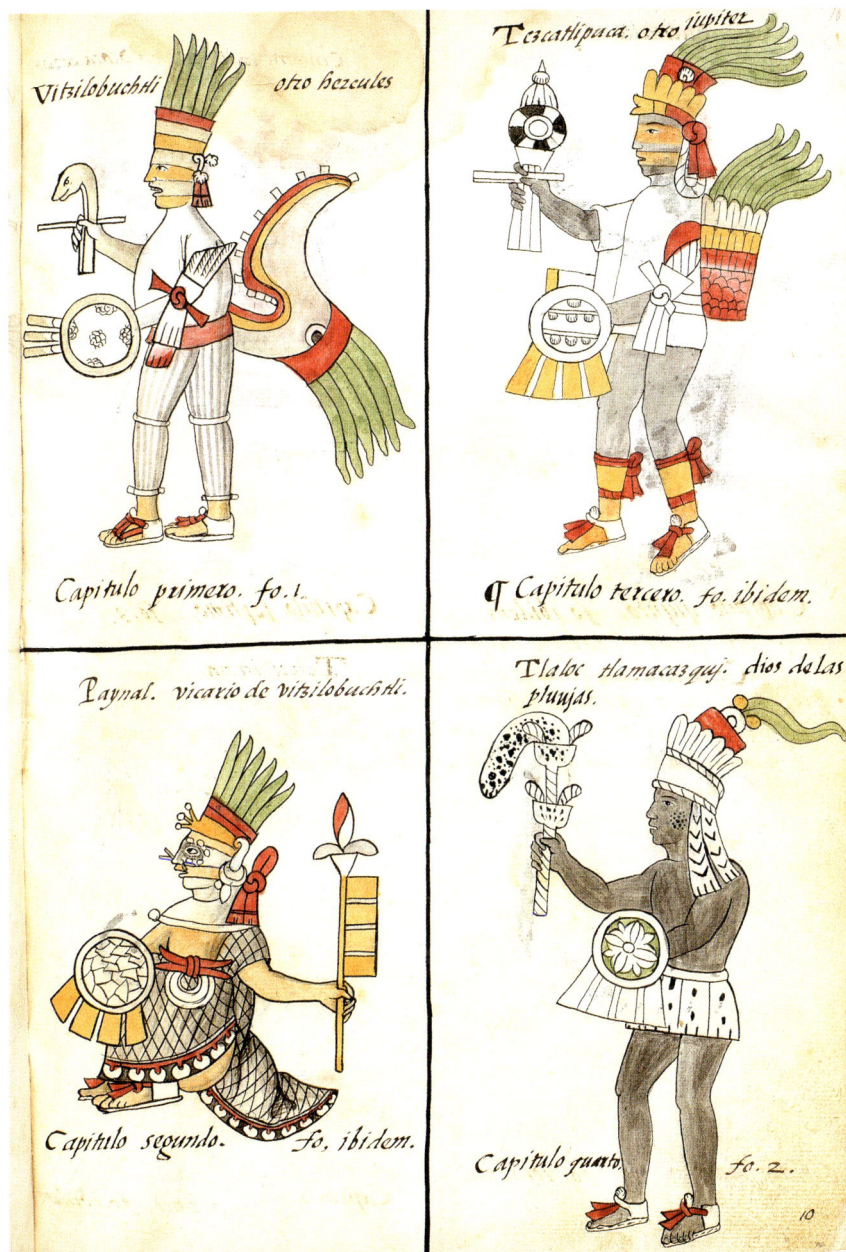

2. Sacrifice

Florence, Biblioteca Medicea Laurenziana, Med. Palat. 218, fol. 84v

> They tied him to the stone, threw him onto it so his shoulders were resting against it and then five of them pinned him down, two for the legs, two for the arms and one for the head. Then the priest who was to kill him came and pierced his chest with a flint-stone he held in both hands, put his hand into the hole and pulled out the heart...

This is how Bernal Díaz del Castillo, a soldier in the service of Cortés, described the human sacrifices that so shocked the Spaniards when they arrived in Mexico. Practised throughout pre-Columbian Meso-America but particularly widespread amongst the Aztecs, sacrifices were offered so that the cosmic cycle—considered to be the result of an endless battle between opposing forces, a daily struggle between the Sun and the Moon, light and shadow, day and night—might continue and the Sun rise every morning.

In a perennial process of regeneration, Aztec gods die and then return to life stronger than before, and it is their death that is 'relived' in the sacrifice. The gods are embodied in the sacrificial victims—their 'images' (*ixiptla*) or representatives—, receiving sustenance from human hearts and blood. This enables them to be reborn, reinvigorated and rejuvenated.

Opposite is an illustration of the sacrifice of the *ixiptla* of Tezcatlipoca, a very important god for the Aztecs. He was embodied by a young man described as "fit, well-disposed and without physical imperfections", who for a year led a life of leisure, learning to play the flute, to drink and to carry "smoking tubes" as "is the custom amongst chiefs and nobles". When the festival of the god drew near, the young man was carefully dressed and adorned, and after various ceremonies taken to the foot of the pyramid where he was to be killed. As he climbed the stairs of the pyramid he destroyed one by one the flutes he had played during the previous year. The victims of the sacrifice were generally soldiers captured in battle, like the *ixiptla* of Tezcatlipoca, but could also be slaves, men found guilty of some crime, young women or children (offered to the deities of the rain and waters).

Another kind of offering was 'self-sacrifice', a ritual practised by the whole population as an act of communication with the gods. This consisted of perforating one's earlobes, lips, tongue, chest, knees or penis with obsidian knives, agave spines, fishbones or bone brooches. These instruments were kept in ceremonial chests called *tepetlacalli*; once bloodied they were offered to the gods by inserting them into grass balls called *zacatapayoli*. The act of self-sacrifice was first performed by the god Quetzalcoatl himself, when he created the human beings of the Fifth Sun (the current one) by mixing blood obtained from his penis with dust made from the bones of humans from the four previous eras ('suns').

Although human blood was the most precious substance of all and hence the offering that most pleased the gods, they also appreciated the sacrifice of animals or offerings of food, precious stones, flowers, clothes and incense.

2. SACRIFICE

Libro · 2.   de las cerimonjas.

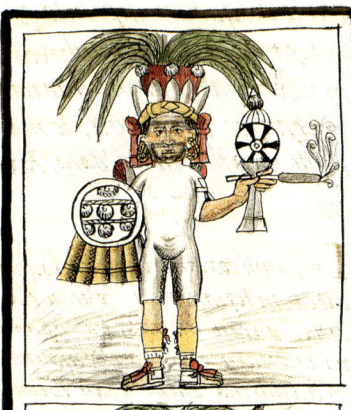

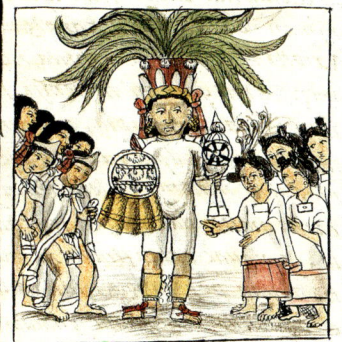

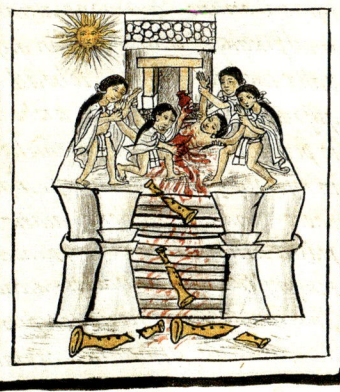

ca muchioa, y na qujn cenca quauh
tic, qujlhujā in cioa: quauhtitin,
quauh chachalan, citlalmaololo:
y naqujn pepenaloia, in teixipla,
atle yiaioca: iuhqujn tlachicotli, iuh
qujn tomatl, iuhqujn telolotli, iuh
qujn quauijtl tlaxixintli, amo qua
cocototztic, quacolochtic, veltzō
melaoac, tzompiaztic, amo ix
quachachaquachtic, amo ixqua
totomonquj, amo ixquaxitonti,
amo ixquaxiquypiltic, amo qua
metlapiltic, amo cuexcochujtztic,
amo quachitatic, amo quapatz
tic, amo quapatlachtic, amo qua
oacaltic, amo quaxozomalacquj,
amo ixquamamalacachtic, amo
ixquatolpopocactic, amo ixqua
tolmemetlapiltic, amo campopo
naztic, amo ixujujlaxtic, amo
canujujlaxtic, amo ixpopotztic,
amo no camachaloacaltic, amo
ixmetlapiltic, amo ixpechtic, a
mo iacapatztic, amo iacacoiac
tic, amo iacaxaxacaltic, amo ia
ca caxtic, amo iacachittoltic, amo
iacauijtoltic, amo iacanecujltic,
can velicac y nijac, iacapiaztic,
amo tenxipaltotomaoac, amo te
xipaltotomac, texipaltomactic,
amo tencaxtic, amono tenmetla
piltic: amono eltzatzacquj, amo
nenepilchanpuchtic, amo nene
pilchacajultic, amo popoloc, amo
tentzitzipi, amo tentzitzipitlatoa

3. Anthropophagy

Florence, Biblioteca Medicea Laurenziana, Med. Palat. 218, fol. 268r

Anthropophagy or ritual cannibalism was also practised sometimes as part of the rite of human sacrifice. It is described in the Florentine Codex in relation to a festival in honour of Xipe Totec, the god of spring and regeneration, and Huitzilopochtli:

> At dawn the prisoners were taken to the temple of Huitzilopochtli ... At the foot of the pyramid the prisoners' captors handed them over to the priests, who grabbed them by the hair and took them up the temple steps ... If they resisted they were dragged to the stone, where they were killed. The heart of each prisoner was ripped out and the bodies thrown down the steps where other priests skinned them ... The hearts were placed in a wooden bowl and offered to the god ... After the bodies had been skinned, they were carried to the *calpulco* ['quarter'] where the captor had made his vow. Here the body was cut up; one thigh was sent to Montezuma for him to eat and the rest was shared out amongst notables and relatives. Usually they went to eat it at the house of the man who had taken the prisoner. The human flesh was cooked up with corn, and each guest received a piece, in a small bowl, with some broth and corn. This dish was called *tlacatlolli*. After eating it they got drunk.

By means of this practice the strength of the enemy was consumed and made one's own, in a kind of communion with the dead person and with the gods. Indeed, cannibalism took on a 'theophagic' significance, in that the sacrificial victim was viewed as the *ixiptla* ('image') of the deity.

The man who had taken the victim prisoner was the only one who did not eat his flesh. Sahagún in fact goes on to say that "the master of the prisoner did not eat his flesh, because he considered it his own, and from the moment he captured him regarded him as a son; likewise the prisoner regarded his master as a father". This suggests the existence of a kind of identification between the sacrificed and sacrificer, as if the prisoner were somehow dying in his master's stead.

3. ANTHROPOPHAGY

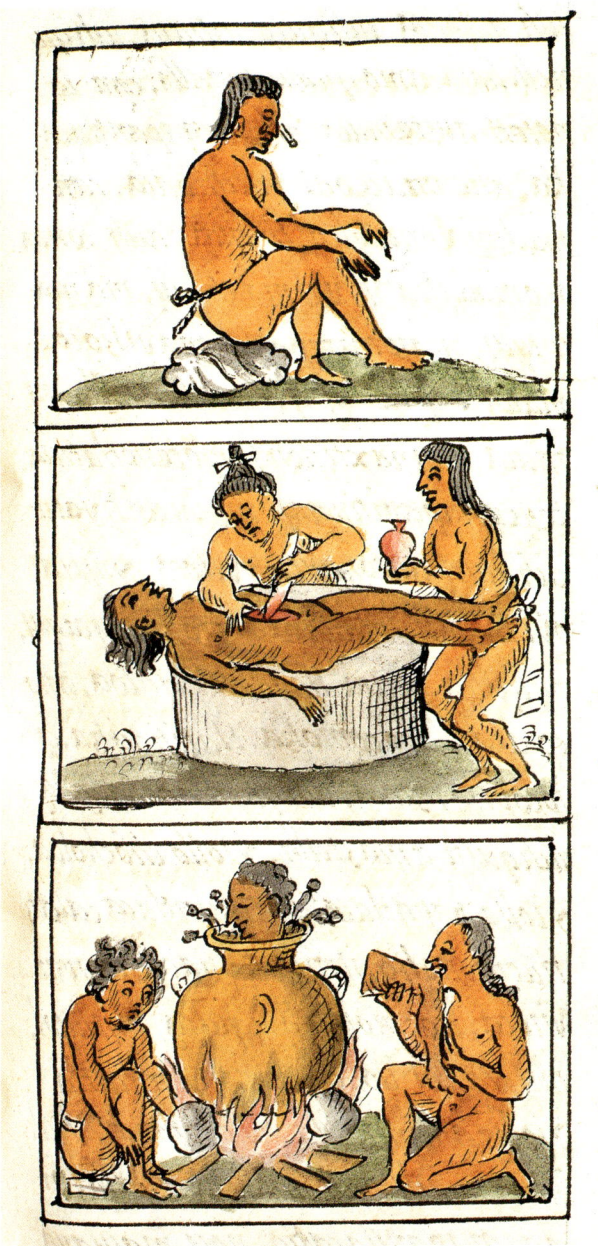

21

4. The *tzompantli*

Florence, Biblioteca Medicea Laurenziana, Med. Palat. 220, fol. 475r

One of the most important structures in the Sacred Precinct of Tenochtitlán was the *tzompantli*, the 'wall (or rack) of skulls'. This was an altar on which human skulls were placed in parallel lines by making a hole at the height of the temples and sticking them onto a pole. Usually the poles were arranged horizontally, although in some cases they were vertical. The base of the structure was also sometimes decorated with skulls alternating with long crossed bones. In Meso-American cities *tzompantli* were often erected near ball-game courts.

The purpose of displaying skulls publicly was to honour the gods, but it was also an explicit manifestation of the political and religious control exercised by the Aztecs over other peoples, given that the skulls were those of prisoners of war sacrificed to the gods. According to some reports, there were about 136,000 skulls on display in the Hueyi Tzompantli of Tenochtitlán (the *tzompantli* of the Sacred Precinct) when the Spanish arrived. Although the nature of the sources suggests this figure was somewhat exaggerated, it is still likely that it was incredibly high. Furthermore, there seem to have been at least five other altars of this kind in the city, although they were presumably smaller.

Bernal Díaz del Castillo, who served under Cortés, recounted that when the Spanish were forced to leave Tenochtitlán in 1520 following a revolt, the Aztecs erected a *tzompantli* to display the heads of the enemy soldiers and animals they had captured. The illustration opposite refers to one of the many battles fought by the Aztecs against the Spanish and their Mexican allies (Tlaxcaltecs, Texcocans, Chalchans, Xochimilcans), during which they took fifty-three prisoners: they "killed them one by one", writes Sahagún, "and tore out their hearts ... First they killed the Spaniards, then all their indigenous friends. After killing them they placed the heads on poles in front of idols ... the Spaniards' highest of all, those of the indigenous people in the middle and the horses' heads at the bottom".

The horses were probably sacrificed and displayed on the altar in the same way as the Spanish soldiers because they too were regarded as brave combatants. The Aztecs had never seen horses before the arrival of the Spanish and were very curious about them, initially believing they were dealing with a single creature consisting of horse and rider.

4. THE 'TZOMPANTLI'

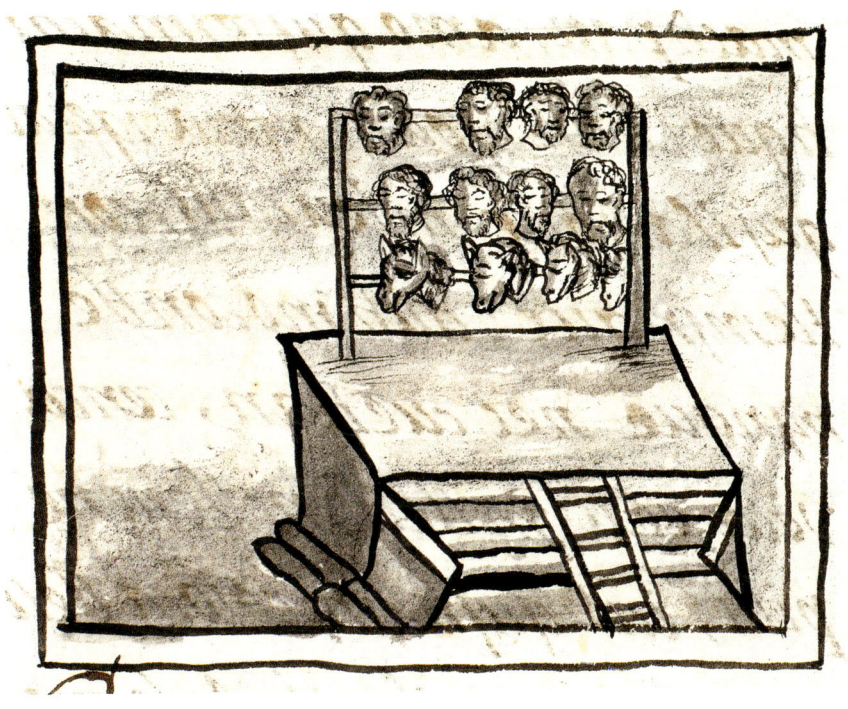

23

5. The Templo Mayor of Tenochtitlán

Florence, Biblioteca Medicea Laurenziana, Med. Palat. 220, fol. 437v

> ...amongst us were soldiers who had been in many parts of the world, to Constantinople, throughout Italy and to Rome, and they said they had never seen such an orderly plaza, so big and with so many people...

This is how Bernal Díaz del Castillo describes the astonishment of the Spaniards when they first saw the central plaza of Tenochtitlán, the heart of the city which consisted of the Sacred Precinct. Here, according to Sahagún, there were seventy-eight buildings, the most important of which was the Templo Mayor, dedicated to Huitzilopochtli and Tlaloc and built in 1325 when the city was founded.

The temple was built in seven different phases over a period of less than two hundred years, with new layers being constructed on top of the previous ones so as to form a kind of onion. From very early on there was a sacrificial stone on the Huitzilopochtli side, while on the Tlaloc side there was a Chac Mool, a statue of a figure with an offering dish in its lap, on which gifts for the gods were placed. The twin temple can be seen in the illustrations opposite: the shrine on the right is devoted to Tlaloc, the one on the left to Huitzilopochtli.

The dual construction had great significance in Meso-American cosmology, symbolizing the two sacred mountains, Tonacatepetl, the Hill of Sustenance, and Coatepec, the Hill of the Snake. The first construction was dedicated to Tlaloc and represented the mountain housing maize and other things that Quetzalcoatl stole from the gods to give to mankind. The second, devoted to Huitzilopochtli, represented the mountain on which the god was born, already an adult and dressed as a warrior, from his mother Coatlicue, who generated him after having placed a feather ball in her lap. On the mountain the god defeated his sister Coyolxauhqui, the Moon goddess, and his four hundred brothers who were jealous of his birth. Once dead, they went to form the Milky Way. In the Meso-American conception of the cosmos, the two pyramids were the place through which it was possible to gain access to the celestial levels and to descend into the underworld; it was the centre of the world's horizontal and vertical planes, the 'navel of the earth'.

Libro duodecimo

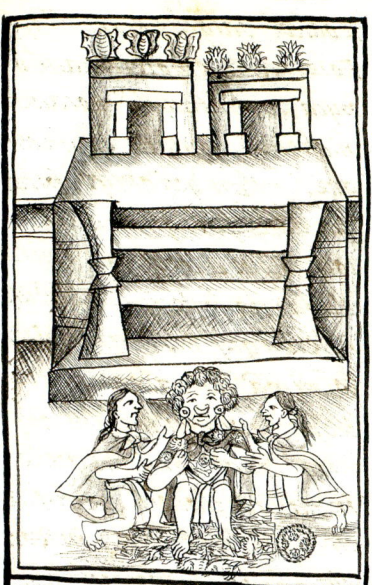

naoch itchpipilcac in vitz naoalotl, teucujtlatl xoxopiltec, tlaxoxopiltectli, yoā yiacapilol, nj̄ stl: Teucujtlatl in tlachiuhtli, tlatzotzontli, yoan tlatzantli, tlacaça oalli, tlateicujololli, noitech pilcaia moteneoa vitznaoaiutl, ixtlan tlatlaan, īyc ixtlan tlatlaan, yncā iiac tzcutli, yoan teuxtli yoā icpac conquetza ivitzitzil naoal: njmā contvqujlia, i tua anecuiotl, hivitl intla chichioalli, njmjltic, achi tzin vitztic, achi tzimpitzauac: njmā ieie mitoz yololli icuex ichtlan incontlalilia ite chpilcac tzivhcuexpalli, yoā itzitzicaztilma, tlatlilpalli macujlcan in tlapotvnjlli, quauh tlachcaiotica, quj molotica, ysan in ytilma in tlanj qujmoquentia, tzō tzō n tecomaio, oo mjcallo: auh in panj qujmolvilia, ysan ixicul: injc tlacujlolli tla quaquallo, camuch incā

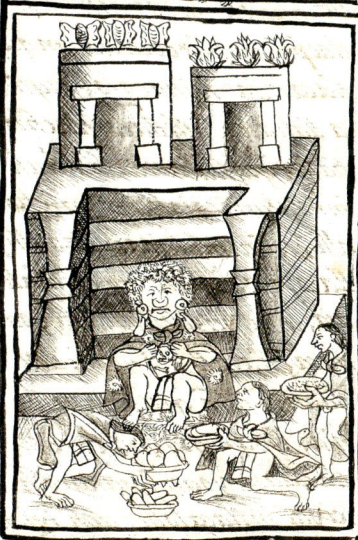

6. Games

Florence, Biblioteca Medicea Laurenziana, Med. Palat. 219, fols. 292v, 269r

The ball game (*tlachtli*) was tied in with the Meso-American view of the cosmos, seen as the product of a clash between opposing but complementary forces such as life and death, day and night, fertility and barrenness, light and darkness. This struggle was reproduced ritually in the game: two teams representing the opposing cosmic forces faced each other on a court which was often shaped like a capital 'I' (opposite, above).

The object of the game was to bounce a heavy rubber ball as many times as possible against the side walls of the court. To do so, the players could use their hips, pelvis and thighs. Part of the game probably also involved getting the ball through rings on the walls and hitting special targets. Sources indicate that the ball bounced very fast and that games could last many hours or even several days. It is likely that the rules varied according to the place and in different periods, but its religious and political significance is unquestionable.

According to Sahagún the ball game, described as one of the "pastimes" of the elite, had lost its religious significance: "rich blankets and gold jewellery, precious stones and slaves were lost and won playing this game". Another of the king's pastimes was "a game similar to that of dice: they painted a cross full of pictures on a mat … and sitting on the mat they took three large beans and let them fall onto the cross … and with this game they lost and won jewels and other things". The exact rules of this game, known as *patolli*, are not known.

6. GAMES

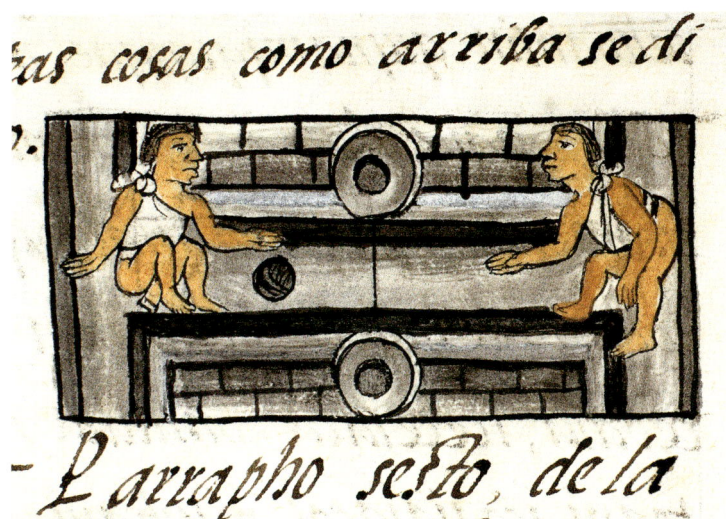

as cosas como arriba se di

l arrapho sesto, de la

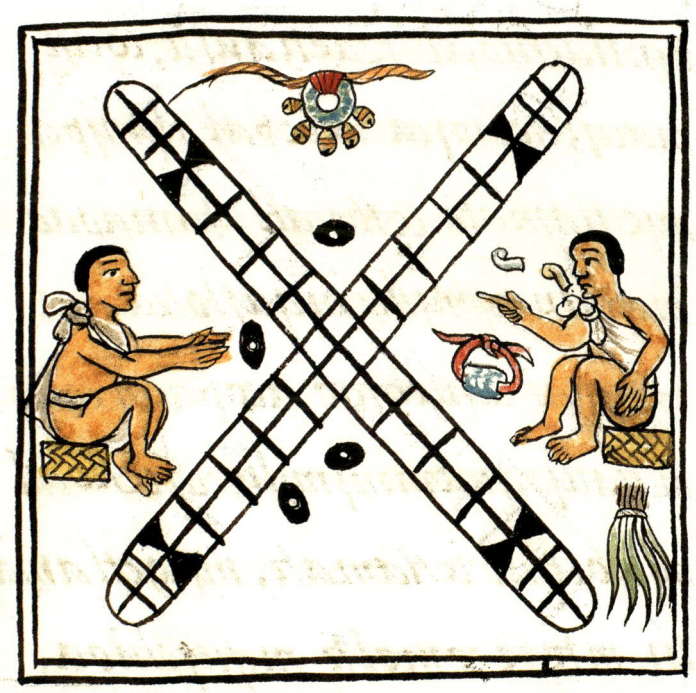

7. Warriors

Florence, Biblioteca Medicea Laurenziana, Med. Palat. 218, fol. 74r-v

War was very important for the Aztec people because it enabled them to exact from subjugated populations the tributes required to satisfy the needs of the large city of Tenochtitlán. Much of the social organization of the Aztecs revolved around war: young boys were educated at school to fight and to be courageous, and practically the only way of rising up the social ladder was to prove oneself to be a brave warrior. In battle, the goal of the soldiers was not to kill the enemy, but to take prisoners, who were grabbed by the hair (opposite, above) and were destined to become sacrificial victims.

The two main groups of warriors in the Aztec empire were the eagle warriors and the jaguar warriors. Both types, clearly recognizable by their dress, can be seen in the picture (opposite, below) illustrating the ceremonies associated with the calendrical cycle. The eagle warriors wore feathers and a helmet in the shape of a bird's head, while the jaguar warriors wore the skin of a jaguar, the head of which acted as a helmet. Typical weapons included a feather-decorated shield and a wooden club edged with obsidian blades.

A warrior who proved himself in battle was called 'eagle-jaguar'. According to Sahagún, the origin of this name lies in the creation myth of the Sun and Moon, in which both animals displayed great courage: the eagle plunged into the great fire immediately after Nanahuatzin and Tecuciztecatl and burnt its feathers, which turned black; next came the jaguar, which was not completely burnt but became spotted.

According to the Aztecs, warriors who died in battle went up to the Sun, as did the victims of sacrifice. They would accompany it from dawn to midday, at which point they were replaced by women who had died during childbirth.

7. WARRIORS

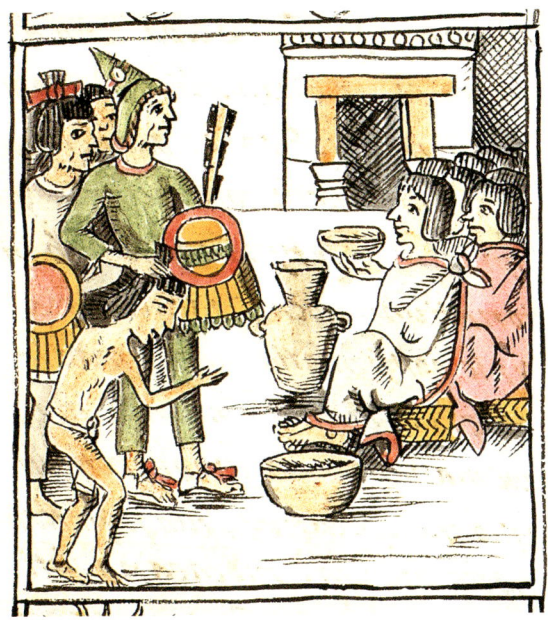

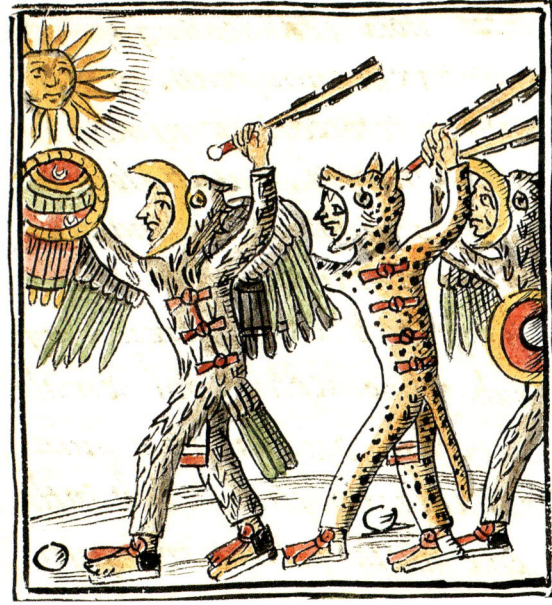

8. The rabbit in the Moon

Florence, Biblioteca Medicea Laurenziana, Med. Palat. 219, fol. 228v

In Mexico it is said that when there is a full Moon it is possible to see a rabbit in it. This visual effect is the result of a combination of dark spots caused by the alternation of rises and craters on the Moon's surface, but the ancient Meso-American peoples had a mythological explanation for it.

Sahagún relates that before the creation of the day, that is the succession of day and night (or of human time), the gods met at Teotihuacán to create the Sun so that it might illuminate the world.

Someone had to sacrifice themselves and the god Tecuciztecatl volunteered. However, another god was also required. Everyone else was afraid and no one stepped forward; so they turned to Nanahuatzin, who was covered with pustules, and he accepted gracefully. Both gods prepared themselves for sacrifice by doing penitence for four days. Tecuciztecatl used feathers, gold and sharp fragments of precious stones and coral as instruments of self-sacrifice, while Nanahuatzin used humble materials and offered up his blood and pus.

A large fire was lit and all the gods gathered round it at midnight. But when the moment came for Tecuciztecatl to throw himself into the fire to be transformed into the Sun he hung back, afraid. Nanahuatzin, on the other hand, threw himself bravely into the fire and began to shine; only then did Tecuciztecatl, who was envious, follow suit. This is how the world came to be illuminated by the Sun to the east (and "its rays spread in all directions"), and then by the Moon, in the order in which Nanahuatzin and Tecuciztecatl had thrown themselves into the flames. But the gods had not reckoned on there being two stars of equal brightness in the sky. So a god took a rabbit and hurled it onto the second sun so as to diminish its brightness. That is why it is possible to see the shape of a rabbit on the face of a full Moon.

However, the legend does not end here: as the Sun did not move, the gods decided to sacrifice themselves so it might rise again thanks to their death. But when all the gods had died (only Xolotl tried to resist), the Sun and the Moon still did not move, and they only stirred into motion with the arrival of the wind, first the Sun and then the Moon. This is why the former illuminates the day and the latter the night.

8. THE RABBIT IN THE MOON

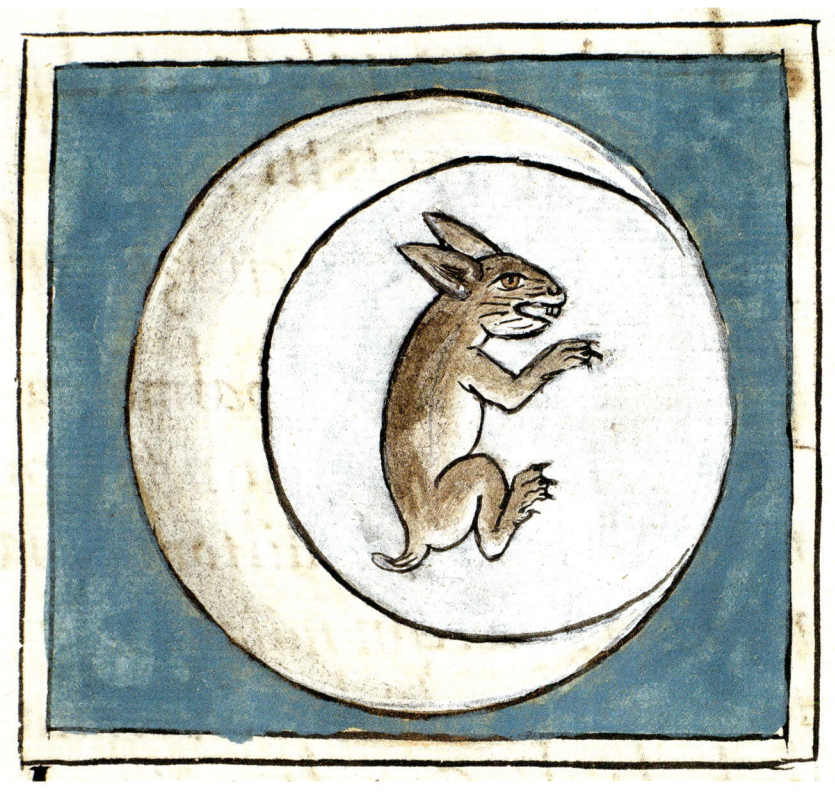

THE WORLD OF THE AZTECS IN THE FLORENTINE CODEX

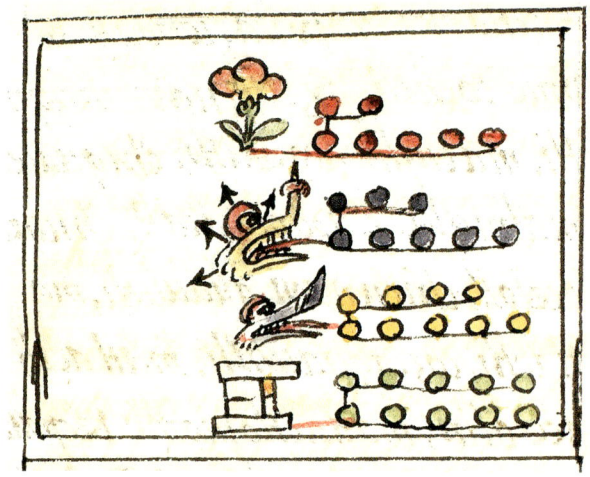

9. The calendar

Florence, Biblioteca Medicea Laurenziana, Med. Palat. 218, fols. 250r, 329r

At least two calendars were used in almost the whole of Meso-America, one solar and the other ritual. The solar calendar had a cycle of 365 days (*xihuitl*) divided into eighteen months of twenty days each (18 × 20 = 360), plus five days considered to be inauspicious, during which it was necessary to avoid any activity whatsoever. On the opposite page is an illustration of the other, ritual calendar (*tonalpohualli*, 'count of days') comprising 260 days, formed by associating the numbers between 1 and 13 with twenty different signs (13 × 20 = 260). The combination of numbers and signs can be seen in the succession of days illustrated in the picture: 1 *cipactli* (Crocodile), 2 *hecatl* (Wind), 3 *calli* (House) ... through to 13 *acatl* (Reed). The numbers then begin again from 1, which is associated with the fourteenth sign, and the series resumes: 1 *ocelotl* (Jaguar), 2 *quauhtli* (Eagle) ... through to 8 *cipactli*, 9 *hecatl* and so on.

In the illustration above are listed days 7 *xochitl* (Flower), 8 *cipactli*, 9 *hecatl* and 10 *calli*; here the number of the day is indicated by the circles. The ritual calendar was principally used by priests (*tonalpouhque*) in divination.

The combination of the solar and the ritual calendars produced a cycle of 52 years (*xiuhmolpilli*), which has been called the 'Meso-American century'. It was always feared that the world would end when the *xiuhmolpilli* did, and to avoid this happening big sacrifices had to be made to the gods. Anyone who survived for a whole *xiuhmolpilli* and had therefore lived through an entire life cycle was considered old and venerable.

9. THE CALENDAR

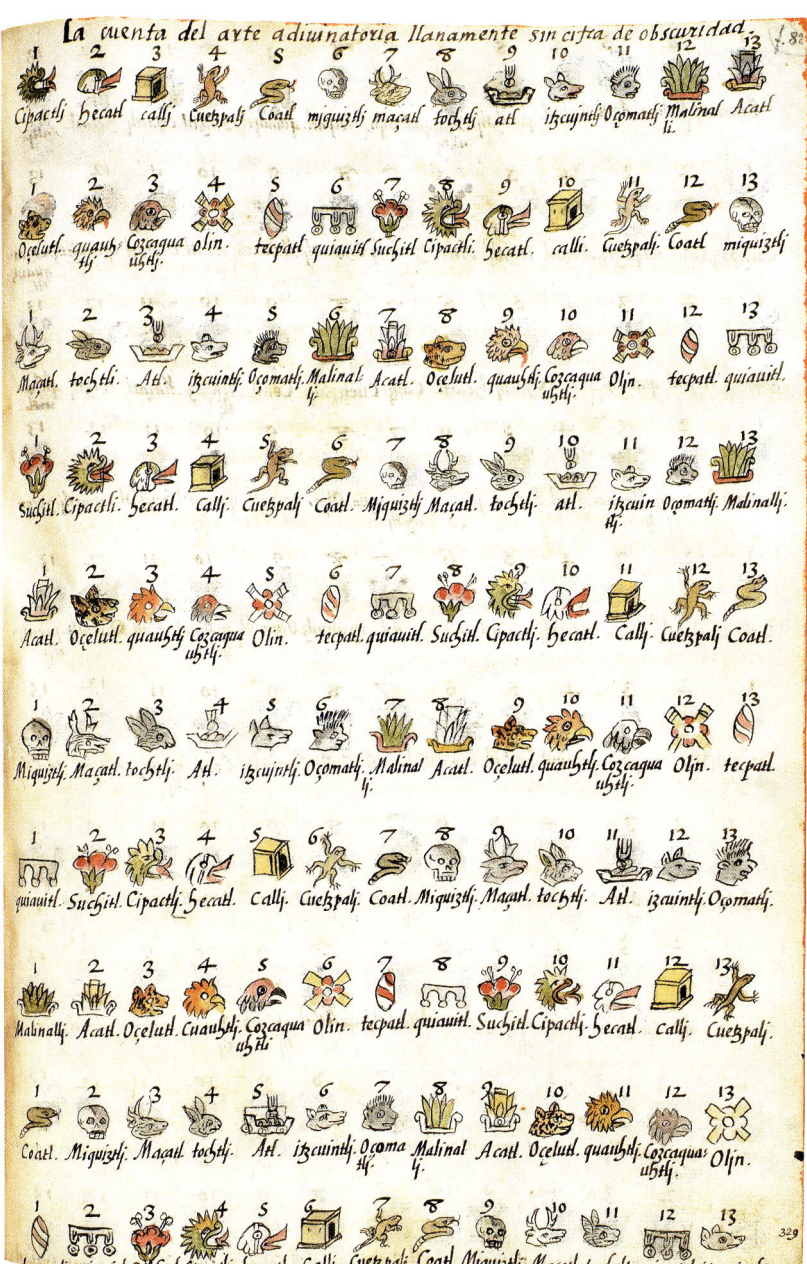

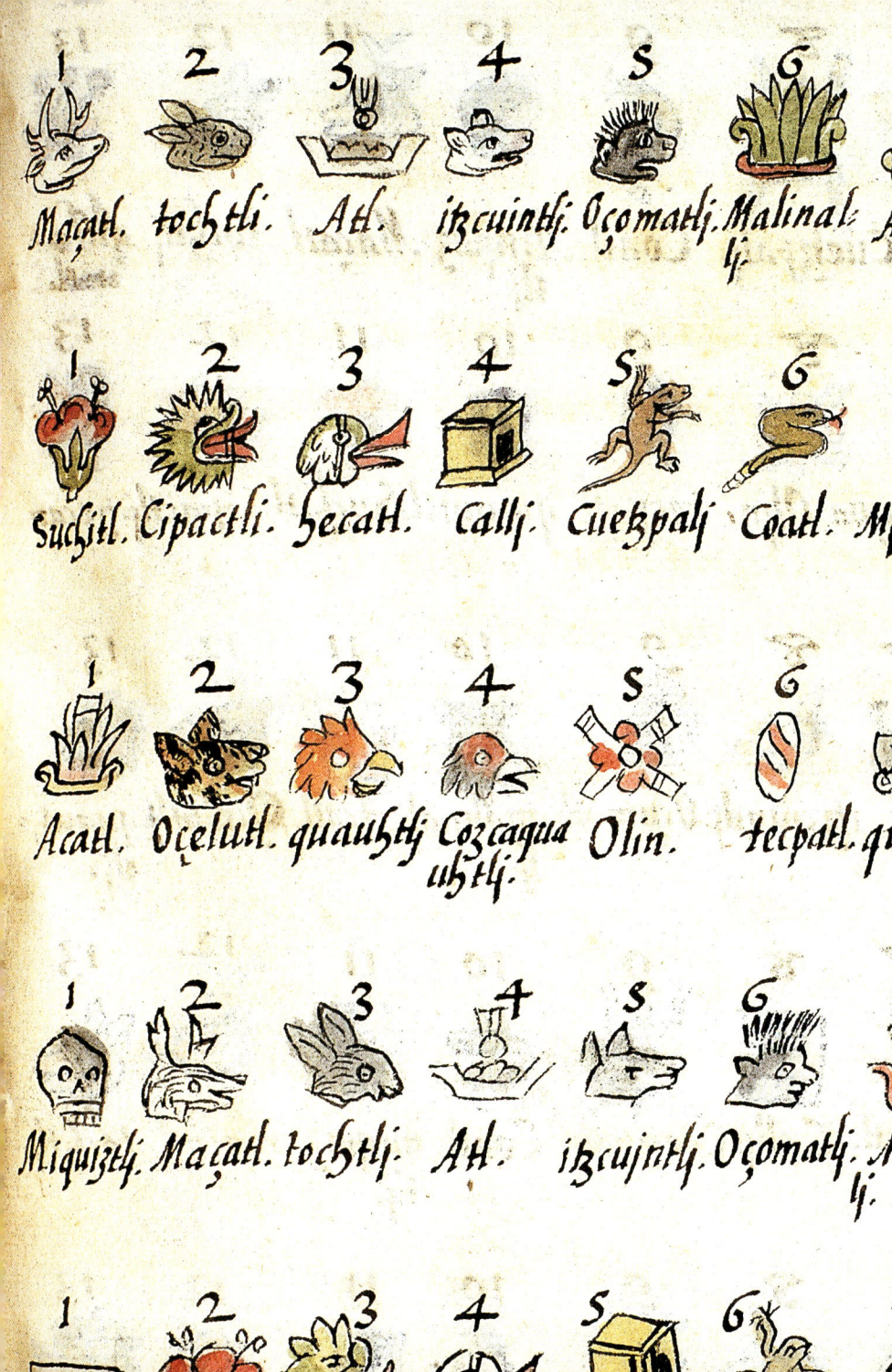

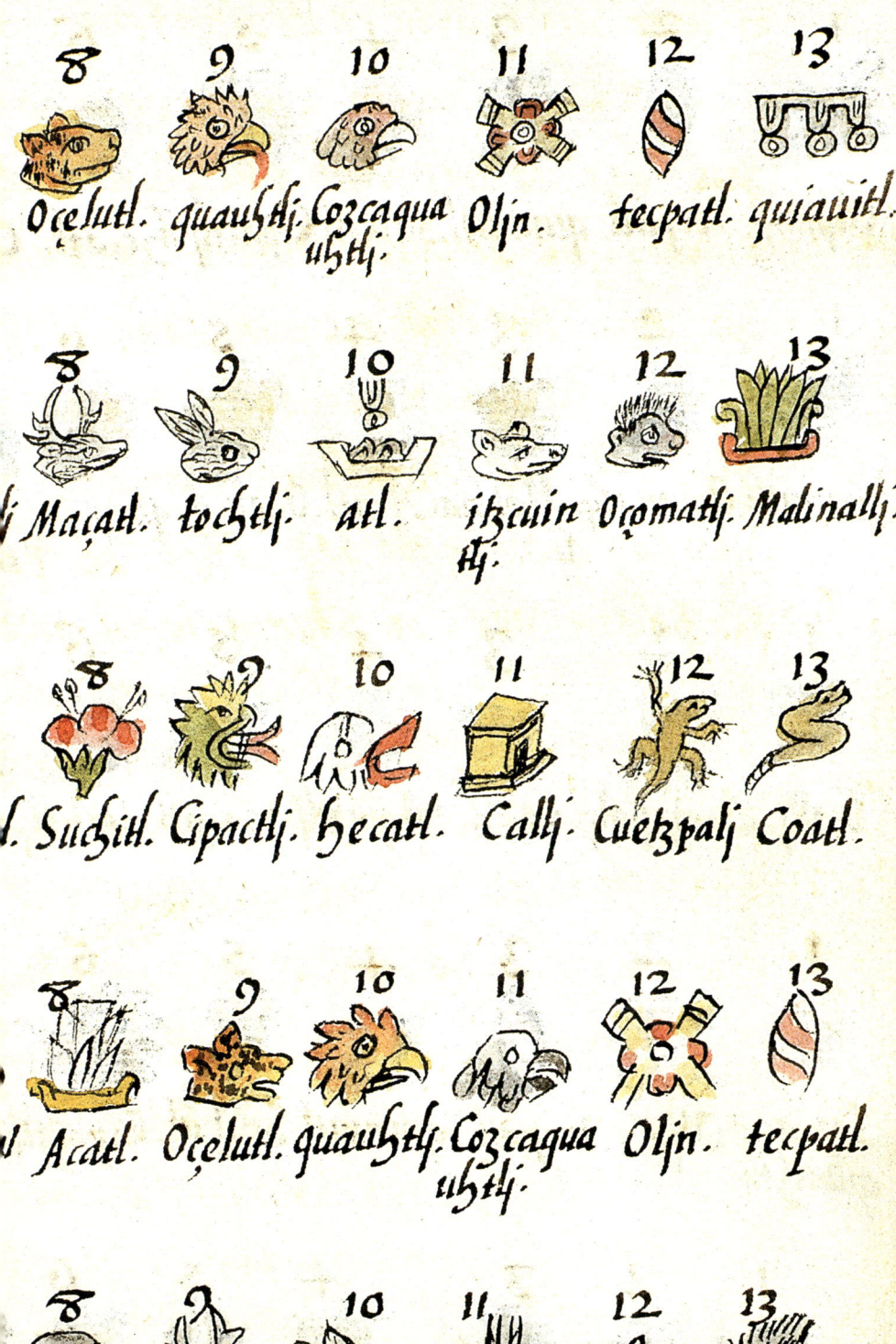

10. 'Baptism' and school

Florence, Biblioteca Medicea Laurenziana, Med. Palat. 218, fols. 275v, 232v

Life in the pre-Columbian period was largely regulated by the calendar: the various farming activities, religious festivals and ritual wars were fixed on the basis of the 'count of days'. The calendar also had a great influence on people's private lives, because it was used to establish important events such as 'baptism' and marriage.

When a baby was born the umbilical cord was cut and buried in the battlefield (if it was a male) or near the hearth (if it was a female). The baby was then purified by washing. The priests chose the name of the child on the basis of the day of birth, which also determined the child's destiny. If a child was born on an inauspicious day, this could be countered by choosing a favourable day for the name-giving ceremony, a kind of baptism during which the child was bathed in water.

As soon as they were born, children were 'offered' by their parents to the temple/school, where they would be educated when they reached an appropriate age. The commoners (*macehualtin*) were sent to the *telpochcalli*, the 'house of the young', where, depending on their age, they swept the temple, gathered wood or assisted soldiers in battle until such time as they were able to become warriors themselves; they also helped potters, builders and farmers in their daily work. The nobles (*pipiltin*), on the other hand, went to the *calmecac*, the 'row of houses', an extremely strict school reserved for the elite, where they received instruction in how to become "those who command, chiefs and senators and nobles, ... those who have military posts"; here the children "serve the gods, perform penitence" and live "humbly and chastely".

10. 'BAPTISM' AND SCHOOL

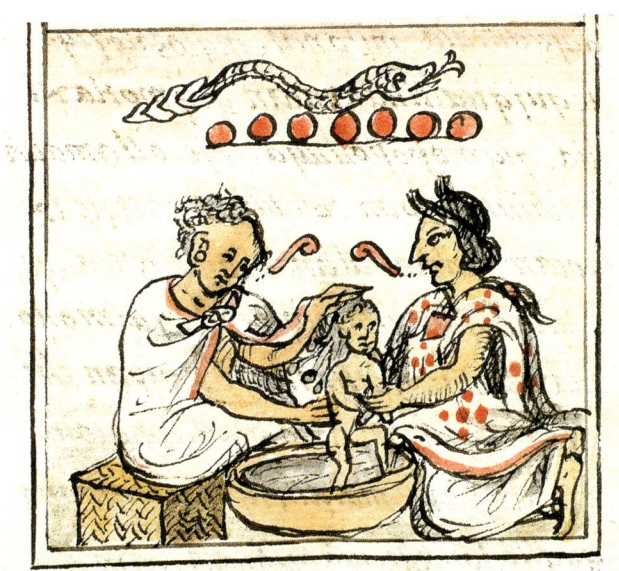

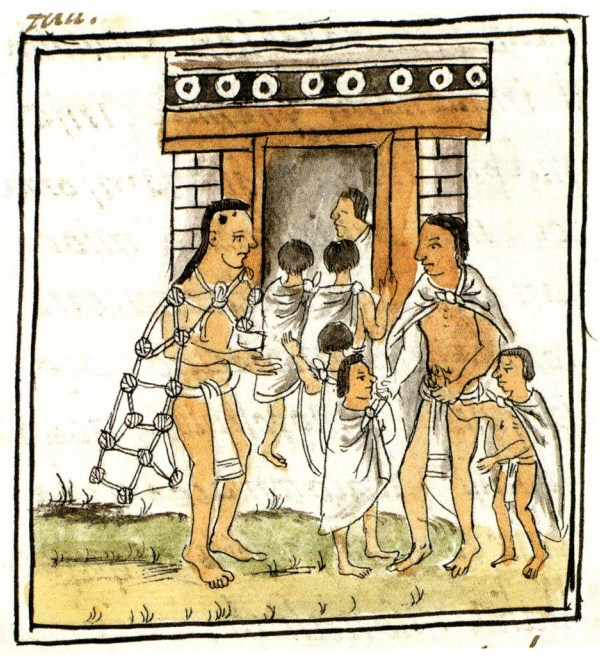

11. Feather art

Florence, Biblioteca Medicea Laurenziana, Med. Palat. 219, fol. 370r

In his *Segunda carta de relación* ('Second Letter of Information') to Charles V, Cortés writes:

> What can be more wonderful than that a barbaric monarch, as he is, should have every object found in his dominions imitated in gold, silver, precious stones, and feathers; the gold and silver being wrought so naturally as not to be surpassed by any smith in the world … and the feather work superior to the finest productions in wax or embroidery.

Feather art or *arte plumario* was one of the most famous of the so-called minor arts practised in pre-Columbian Meso-America. The artisans who devoted themselves to it (*amanteca*) were called, together with goldsmiths and sculptors, 'Toltecs', since they were considered the heirs of the people that had passed down the arts and trades to the Aztecs. Their task was to mould divine substance into physical materials, given that, as Sahagún says, "they have god in their heart". There were special featherworking schools where boys "acquired a good eye and heart and the skill of the artisan" and girls learnt to do "manual jobs and to dye well".

Objects were made by sketching a preliminary design onto a paper support made from agave and tree bark and then attaching the feathers to it. According to Sahagún the *amanteca* needed to be "imaginative, diligent, faithful … skilled in arranging and gluing the feathers, and also, as they are of different colours, embellishing the work; and finally, very skilled in affixing them properly". The feathers came from various bird species and a range of different colours and sizes were used; the most highly valued of all were those of the quetzal, a small bird native to tropical forest environments, which has a limited number of very long tail-feathers that were used principally for headpieces.

Feather-art products were reserved for the Aztec elite—the king, nobles, priests and warriors—who wore them principally for ceremonies. Items included cloaks, fans and headpieces or diadems, such as Montezuma's celebrated Penacho (feather crown), housed in the Museum of Ethnology in Vienna.

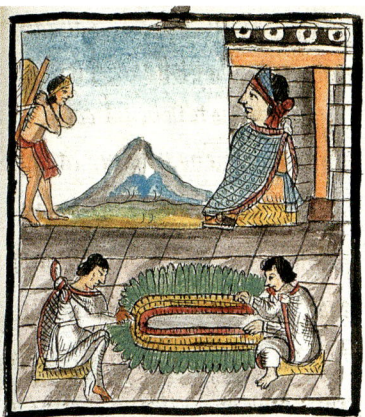

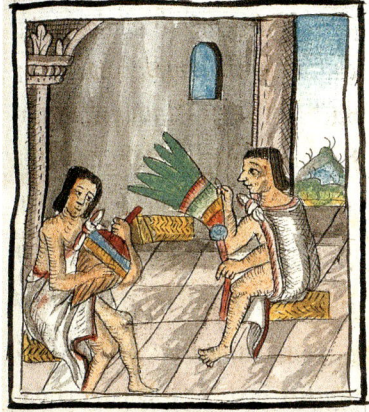

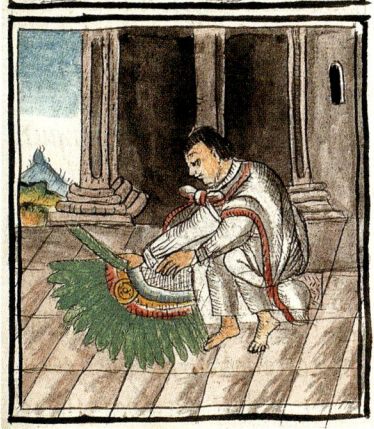

mochi tlaçoihuitl uel ipan tlapiuis:
icnonqua quintecac, quincaltin cen
tetl calli quinmacac iniscoian itlama
tecahoan catca imitech pouia: nepanis
toca intenochtitlan amanteca joan
intlatilulco amanteca. Auh miehoan
tin, canquiscahuiaia mquichioaia
itlatqui vitzilobuchtli inquitoca
iotiaia teuquemitl, quetzalquemitl
uitzitzilquemitl, xiuhtotoquemitl,
ictlatlacuilolli, ictlatlamachilli
iniemochi inizquican icac tlaçoihuitl. yoan quichioaia miscoian
itlatqui motecuçoma: mquinmaca-
ia, mquintlauhtiaia icoahoan in
altepetl ipan tlatoque, icmonotzaia
motenehoaia tecpan amanteca
itlultecahoan in tlacatl. Auh mce
quintin, motenehoaia calpiscan
amanteca, itechpouia inizquitetl
icaca icalpiscacal motecuçoma:
iehoatl quichioaia, intlein imaceh
uallatqui motecuçoma inipan ma
cehoaia, mitotiaia: inicoac ilhuitl
quiçaia, quitlatlattitia, quitlane
nectiaia, mçaço catlehoatl queleuiz
inipan mitotiz: caceentlamantli
iecauia, cecentlamantli quichioaia

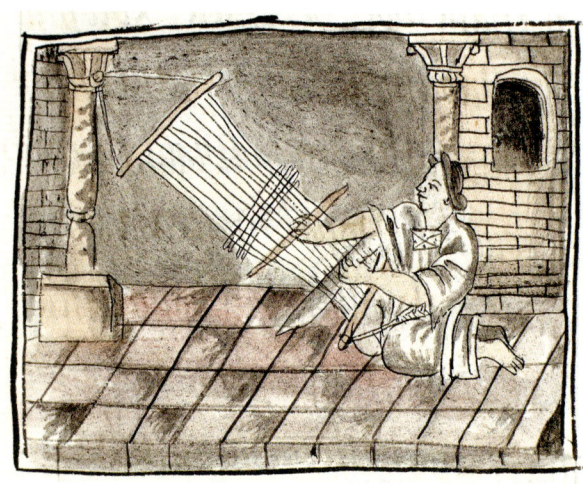

12. The loom

Florence, Biblioteca Medicea Laurenziana, Med. Palat. 220, fol. 26r; 219, fols. 281v, 280v

> The spinner knows how to use the whorl and spindle, and how to unthread what is old. A good spinner produces fine, well-twisted thread … The weaver produces the warp and puts it into the loom … A good weaver tightens and beats what she weaves and straightens what has been poorly woven with a thorn or needle, and makes fabric of an adequate thickness or thins out an over-thick one. She also knows how to insert the fabric into the loom and lengthen it to measure … she also knows how to produce the weft of that fabric. A bad weaver is lazy, inattentive, a poor worker, he damages what he weaves, makes poor fabric and what he weaves is thin … The tailor knows how to cut, respect measurements and sew clothes well…

This is how Sahagún describes the artisans responsible for making clothes for the Aztec population. In reality, family needs were mainly met by women who carried out the task at home. They used the so-called backstrap loom, in which the threads were attached at one end to an upright pole and at the other to a kind of belt strap that went round the woman's back at waist height. However, some women did spinning and weaving on more than just a domestic basis, making the *huipil,* a typical woman's blouse, and blankets, which were traded and used as currency or for paying taxes.

The majority of the Aztec population could only wear clothes made from agave yarn, undyed and without any adornment, while the nobles wore coloured cotton clothes decorated with shell or bone-and-feather patches.

12. THE LOOM

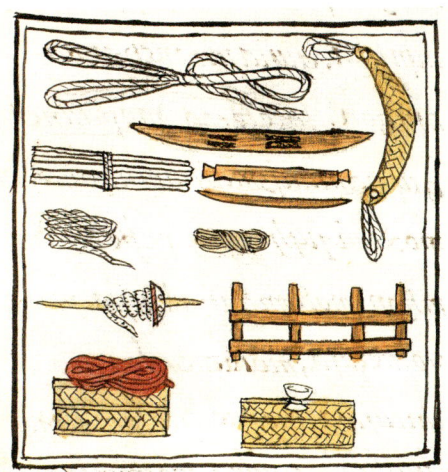

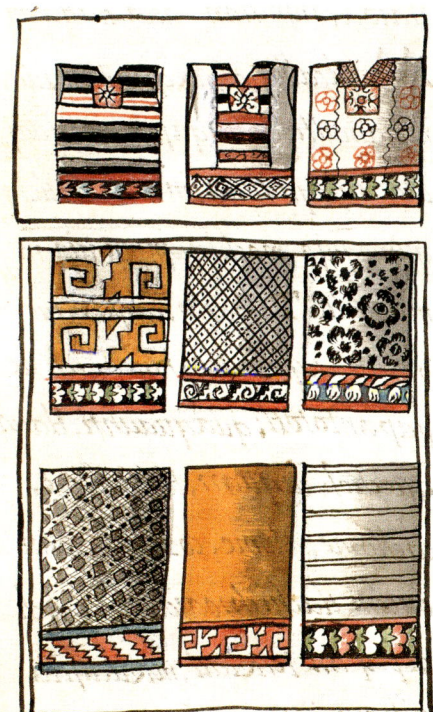

13. Merchants

Florence, Biblioteca Medicea Laurenziana, Med. Palat. 219, fol. 316r

One of the more important groups in Aztec society was that of the *pochteca*, merchants who undertook long journeys in search of precious commodities and goods. Organized into guilds, the *pochteca* were not bound by the laws governing the lives of the majority of citizens. Their influence was due not just to the rare products they procured but also to the information they were able to gather in the lands they visited. Given that they made trips to little-known regions, they were often entrusted with diplomatic missions or asked to explore new territories with a view to a possible war of conquest. Sahagún comments that "if they had to venture into lands that were at war [with the Aztecs], first they learnt the language of that people, then they imitated their dress so as to appear indigenous rather than foreign". Merchants could be recognized by the sticks they carried, like their god Yiacatecuhtli, and by their feather fans.

As pack animals and the wheel were unknown to Meso-America, goods were carried on foot by *tlameme* (porters); they placed their load in a wooden frame (*cacaxtli*), supporting the weight with a cord that went round the porter's forehead and shoulders. In the illustration opposite (centre) the footprints indicate the path taken by the *tlameme*.

Before the departure of the *pochteca*, big banquets were organized in their honour and offerings made to the gods as a request for protection during their journey. If the trip was a success, these ceremonies were repeated upon their return to thank the gods, and during the banquets some of the goods they had acquired during their travels were shared out amongst the guests. One of the typical items distributed were cacao beans, which were used both to make chocolate and as currency. In fact there was no coinage as such in Meso-America; instead they used certain particularly valuable and manageable goods as a form of currency.

The *pochteca* lived principally in Tlatelolco, near Tenochtitlán, its twin city. Here there was a large market that greatly surprised the Spaniards when they first saw it, for the range of goods on sale, the orderly layout and the general organization. Sahagún describes it as follows: "It was so big that just one day was not sufficient to visit it all; it was surrounded by porches and shops, and there were houses where three judges settled disputes, with the help of other officials whose job it was to examine the goods…" Every conceivable kind of product was sold there, ranging from basic essentials to luxury goods from distant lands; amongst the many people that worked in the market there were butchers, cacao tradesmen and female cooks.

13. MERCHANTS

ellos muchas otras alhajas y atavíos, para su proprio trato y rescate, ansí atavíos de hombres como de mugeres ansí para principales como para comunes; como se cuenta en la letra.

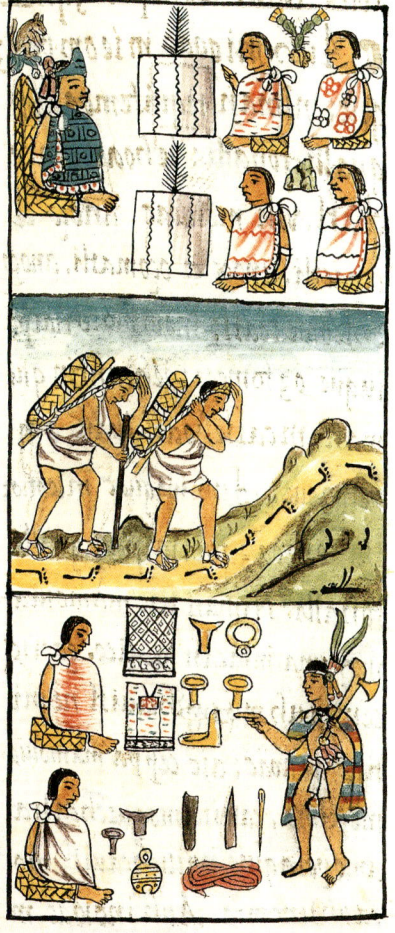

Hatocamaxtlatl iacauiac, ioan tlamachcueitl, tlamachhuipilli. Ini tlatquitl uel iscoian, iasca, mduitzotzin. Auh izcatqui mean imiscoian mtlatqui puchteca, inic onoz tomecati, onteeunenemi, tepeio, teuuitlatl: iuhquin tlatocaiotl, ican teuuitla isquaamatl, ioan chaiaoac cozcatl, teuuitlatl, ioan teuuitla nacochtli; ioan teuuitlatl. Hatza qualoni, intech monequi manaocacihoa: iehcantin incihoapipilti, icquitzacoa minnacaio, ioan in maxtlaztli, mitoca matza tzaztli: ioan teuuitlanacochtli, ioan teuilonacochtli. Auh incan maceoaltin intech monequi; iehoatl imiz nacochtli, amochitl, ioan itztlaeoalli neximaloni, ioan uitzauhqui itztli, ioan tochomitl, ioan uitzmallotl, ioan coiolli. O ca isquichin, inic mochichioaia, inimiscoian in tlatqui m

14. Cacao and chocolate

Florence, Biblioteca Medicea Laurenziana, Med. Palat. 220, fol. 71v

In a letter to Charles V, Cortés described cacao beans as "a fruit resembling the almond, that is sold after being ground, and is held in such estimation that it is used as money throughout the country, and employed in purchases in the markets and everywhere else". From cacao beans (*cacahuatl*) they also obtained a precious liquid, namely chocolate (*xocolatl*). The story goes that over two thousands jugs of cocoa were served at the banquet celebrating the coronation of Montezuma, and during the meals organized to celebrate the return of merchants from their travels "a very good cocoa, mixed with spices" was served. Guests also received cacao beans with which to make chocolate and tortoise-shell mixing spoons.

The process of making chocolate is illustrated opposite: cacao beans were toasted on a cooking plate (*comal*), then shelled and ground up. The resulting paste was diluted with hot water, and spices, vanilla or honey were added as flavourings, since neither sugar nor milk were known to the Aztecs. The froth obtained by pouring the chocolate from high up into a pot on the ground was a measure of its excellence. Montezuma, for instance, "after he had finished eating, normally drank a kind of chocolate in his own particular fashion, with the cocoa being whipped up so it was more froth than cocoa".

The beverage made from pure cacao and spices was considered the greatest delicacy, and was destined for the nobles. According to Bartolomé de las Casas, "it was a point of honour amongst the Aztec lords, nobles and warriors not to drink wine. The customary drink was cocoa and other beverages made from toasted corn flour, which were not inebriating but refreshing and strengthening. The drink reserved for the commoners was made from a mixture of cacao beans and those of other plants, especially corn". Sahagún writes:

> The drinking-cocoa seller grinds up the beans like this: the first time he splits open and breaks up the beans; the second time he grinds them up a bit more; and the third and last time he grinds them up finely and mixes them with grains of corn that have been washed and cooked. Thus ground and mixed, he pours in water into a cup; if he pours in just a little water, he makes a good cocoa; if a lot, there is no froth. To make it well, the following rules have to be observed: it must be filtered and strained, after which it is poured back and forth, which makes the froth rise ... Sometimes it becomes too thick and is mixed with water after grinding. Those who know how to make good cocoa sell it made well and good just like the nobles drink it, smooth and frothy, reddish, coloured and pure, without too much paste ... Poor-quality cocoa has lots of paste and water and therefore does not produce froth.

Cocoa was also believed to be hallucinogenic. Sahagún reports that it was regarded as a "fungus" because it "inebriates and intoxicates". Moreover, "if a commoner drank it he was considered wicked ... Only the king, the nobles and the great warriors drank it".

14. CACAO AND CHOCOLATE

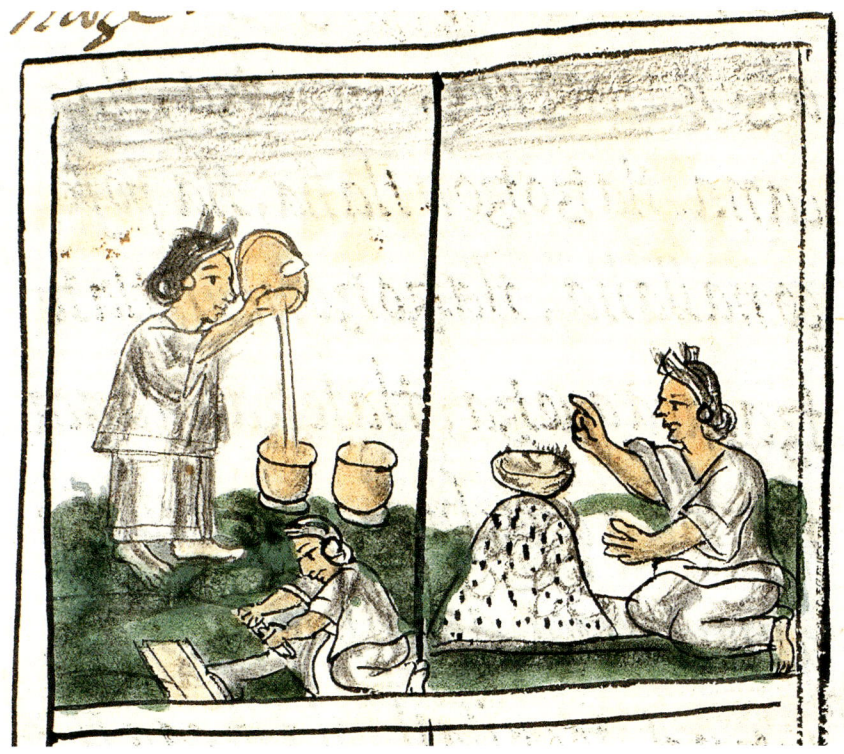

15. *Pulque*

Florence, Biblioteca Medicea Laurenziana, Med. Palat. 218, fol. 52r

The alcoholic beverage drunk by the Aztecs was *octli*, better known as *pulque* (thought by some to be a word of Antillean origin) and produced by fermenting *aguamiel*, the sap of the agave, or maguey, plant. Sahagún observes:

> In the past the wine or *pulcre* of this land was considered evil due to its negative effects, because when they were drunk, some people threw themselves off the mountainside, others hanged themselves, jumped into the water and drowned, committed murder. And they attributed all this to the god of wine and to wine, not to the drunk … they did not consider what they did while drunk to be sinful, even if very serious sins were involved.

In actual fact the Aztecs had numerous rules and laws intended to discourage excessive consumption of the beverage, a likely sign that there was considerable abuse. The elderly—those who were at least fifty-two years old and had therefore survived an entire cycle of the calendar—were the only ones allowed to drink *pulque* without restriction. The rest of the population was permitted to consume it on special occasions like religious festivals, 'baptisms' and weddings, and only rarely was drunkenness tolerated. If young commoners were found drunk, they were publicly beaten up as an example to others; nobles received the same treatment, but away from the public gaze. For an adult, getting drunk in normal circumstances could lead to the confiscation of all his goods and property ("he who loses control of himself does not deserve to have a house, but to live like an animal in the fields") or even public execution.

An indication that drunkenness was considered undesirable is that when the gods gave *pulque* to humans, they warned them never to drink more than four cups of it. The god of 'wine' depicted in the illustration opposite is Tezcatzoncatl, described by Sahagún as "a kind of Bacchus". However, there were many *pulque* deities, known collectively as the *Centzon Totochtin* or '400 rabbits'. Sahagún attributes the name to the fact that there are "many different ways of getting drunk" with *pulque*. The festival of one of the *pulque* gods was on day *ome tochtli*, '2 Rabbit', during which everyone drank with straws from a large jar that was topped up continually. Sahagún also reports that the Aztecs believed children born on this day were destined to become "drunkards, prone to drink wine, and who seek nothing else in life except wine".

15. 'PULQUE'

blo qujnvicaz ynjmanjma.

G. Ocnoce diablo, qujmoteutitiaque

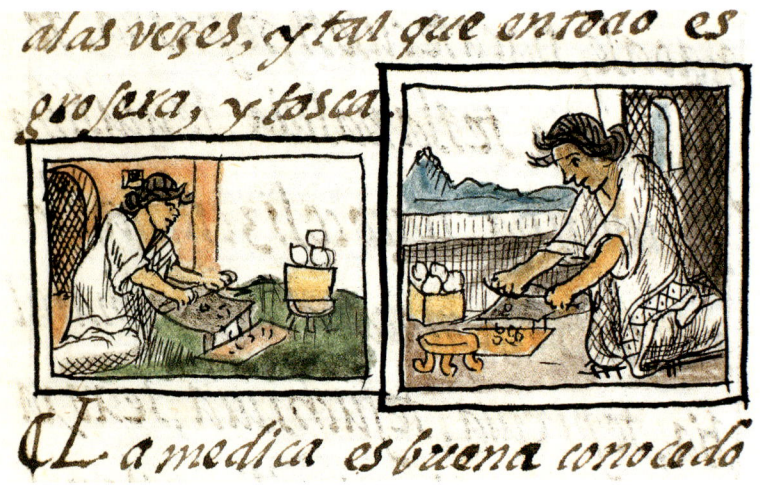

16. Agriculture and food preparation

Florence, Biblioteca Medicea Laurenziana, Med. Palat. 220, fol. 40r; 218, fol. 315r

The Aztec economy was based mainly on agriculture. Farming was the responsibility of the commoners (*macehualtin*), who cultivated land assigned to them and that of the nobles and ruler. Their taxes were paid in kind, in the form of produce or working days. Each head of family had a patch of land (*milpa*) that he could leave to his children and which he was obliged to look after and cultivate personally with the help of labourers; if he did not, or if he committed a serious crime, his land could be confiscated. When a young couple married, they received a plot of land from the quarter (*calpulli*) in which they lived.

The staple crop was corn (opposite), from which the Aztecs made a kind of bread. As the plough was unknown to them, they planted their crops by placing seeds in holes made in the ground with a stick (*coa*). On their *milpa* they also grew *tomatl*, *chilli* and squash.

Preparing food (above) was the task of women, who started learning to cook for the whole family from a very early age, performing increasingly complex tasks as they grew older. They had the job of softening the corn by cooking it with slaked lime and then grinding it. "The woman who knows how to cook well must be able to do the following things ... make *tortillas*, prepare the dough ... taste whether foods are good or not ... make every kind of dish, and must also be clean".

While the *macehualtin* had a very simple diet, the elite ate richer and more abundant fare. Sahagún produces an endless list of dishes flavoured with different sauces made from chillies, tomatoes and squash seeds, and describes in great detail the legendary banquet held to celebrate the coronation of Montezuma.

16. AGRICULTURE AND FOOD PREPARATION

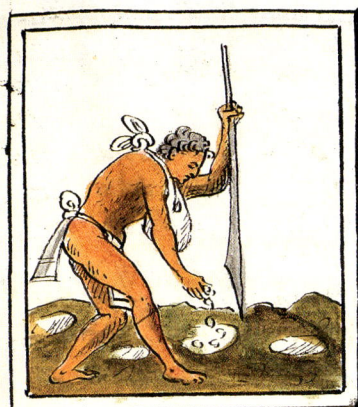

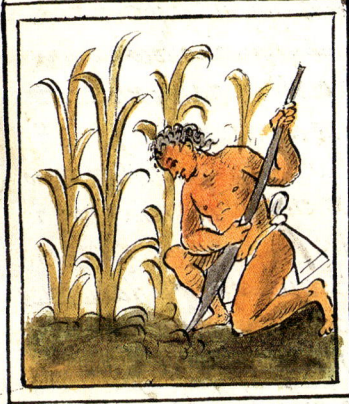

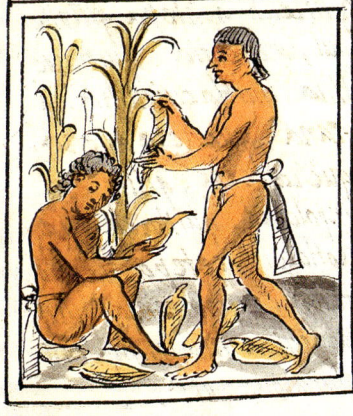

elmiquinj, cacamo, cacamoanj,
ixquich quitoca, ontlatzpeoa, y
nimilpan, ymimilco ymi cuentla,
auh ynoixchoac, iniepapatlacatoc,
ytec, tlapupuxoa, tlatlalhuja, tla
cuentlapana, ixtlalilhujuhtire
mj; auh intlaamilli, cā atla
xilia. auh intlachiname, chi
nāpanecatl, cintamaloa, cinta
malaquja, chilteca, chilque
tza, tlacoquipachoa, ie vncarin
inquitta, ynamonenvetzi, ymi
ciavis, yrinecôcol, ymje quitta
ynecuiltonol, yne iollalilis, yno
tlamuchiuh ynoquittac itona
caiouh, moiollalia, paqui, vel
lamati, tlacalaquia, ixquich
quicalaquja ymicin iniauitl,
yniztac, incoztic, inxiuhtoc
tli. auh iniquac pixca, intlacui
cuj nononqua quitema, quica
quixtia, quipepena, inveuej
cintli, cequi cochollalia, coochol
lalia, cequi colchicaloa, yca
lixquac quj pipiloa ymiochol, y
mi olchical, iuh qujntlapipilac
ocholli, ynolchicalli. auh inmā
quitl nonqua quitema, yoan
impopoiotl atleguixcaoa, tlacē
toca much cohoia, ymizquitatl

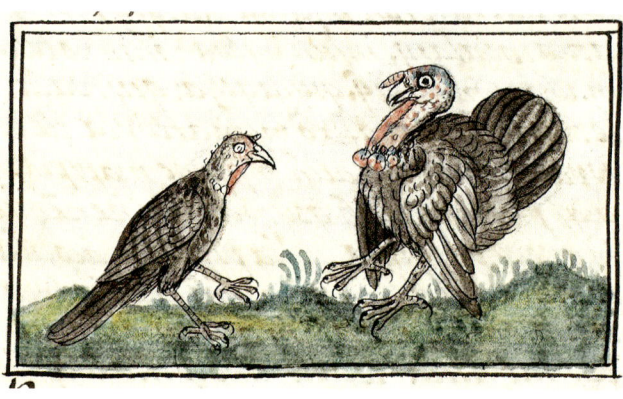

17. Fauna

Florence, Biblioteca Medicea Laurenziana, Med. Palat. 220, fols. 208v, 209r, 213v;
p. 52: 155v, 217r, 198v (left column), 173v, 178r, 177v, 177r, 198v (right column);
p. 53: 215r, 222r, 220r, 216r (left column), 253v, 256r, 259v (right column)

After having dealt with higher beings and humans, Sahagún moves on to "natural things", that is animals and plants. Thanks to this part of his work important information has survived about the Meso-American animal and plant kingdoms and the way in which local populations exploited natural resources.

Before the discovery of the Americas, many of the animals reared in Europe—cows, pigs, chickens, hens, horses—were unknown to the Meso-American peoples. Instead they raised rabbits, *xoloitzcuintli* (a breed of hairless dog), birds and in particular turkeys, the meat of which is highly praised by Sahagún. They supplemented their diet with wild boars, deer, tapirs, birds, which they hunted with nets (opposite, bottom), plus frogs, ants, crickets, agave larvae and snakes. Other animals were hunted chiefly for their skins, such as the jaguar and other felines, or for their feathers. When on a hunt, it was necessary to ask the gods for permission to kill an animal, and the number of 'victims' had to be commensurate with the hunter's needs, otherwise he would be punished.

An explanation of the origins of some animals and their characteristics can be found in the creation myth of the Sun and Moon. When the stars were created and began to move, some things were fixed for ever; for instance, the horns that the rabbit had temporally lent to the deer remained with the latter, while the shoes that slipped off the feet of the birds as they flew off became sea stars, and so on.

On the following pages are some pictures from Book 11 depicting mammals (jaguar and armadillo), birds (quetzal, hummingbirds, parrots, birds of prey and crows), reptiles, amphibians, fishes (some of which imaginary) and insects (locusts, larvae, mosquitoes).

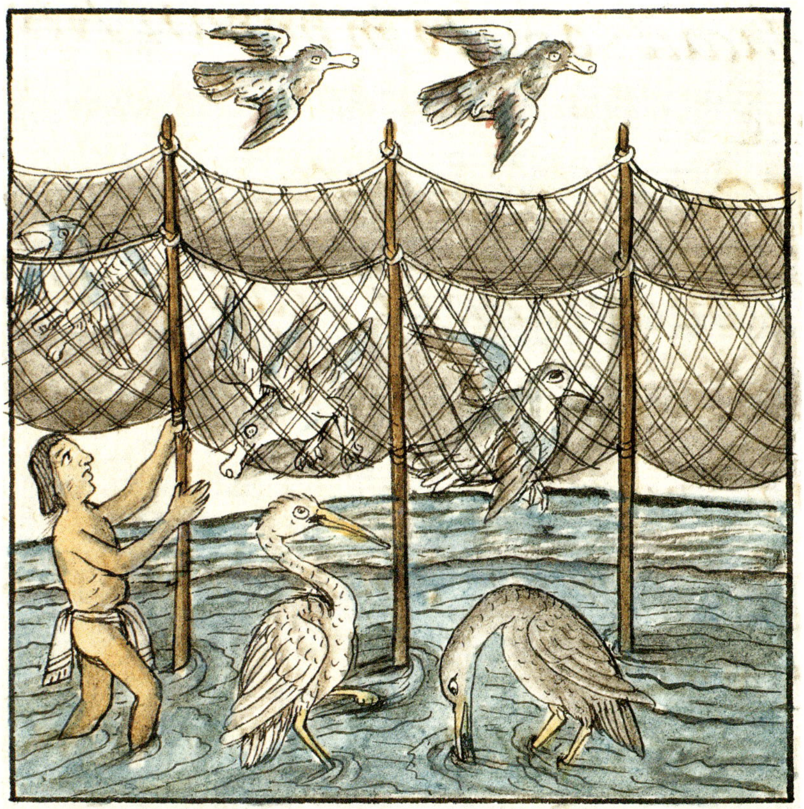

17. FAUNA

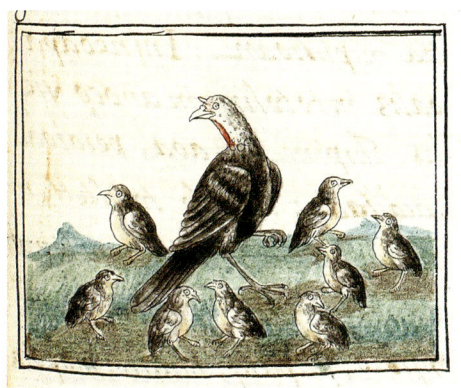

51

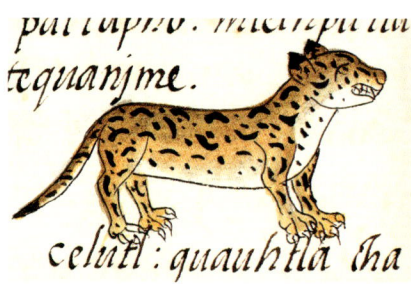

ocelutl: quauhtla tlaca

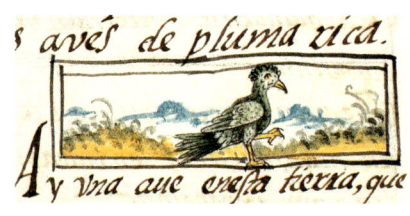

aves de pluma rica.

Ay vna aue enesta tierra, que

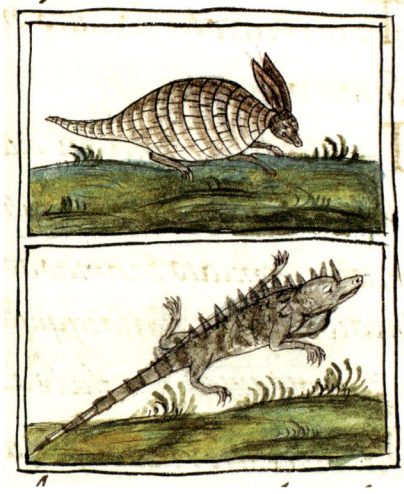

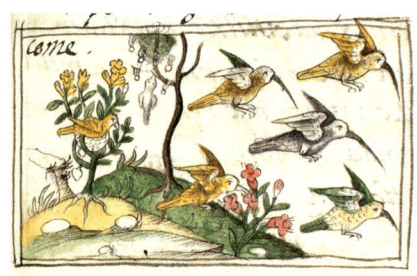

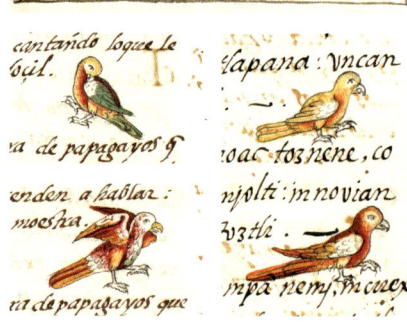

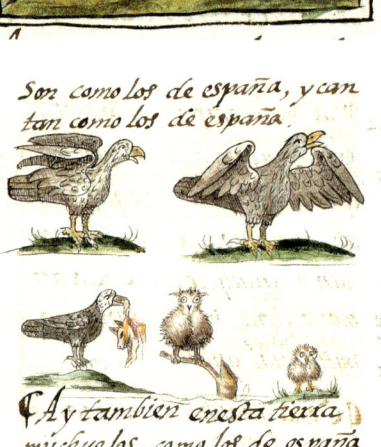

Son como los de españa, y can
tan como los de españa.

¶ Ay tambien enesta tierra
muchos buhos, como los de españa
llaman los quauhtecolotl.

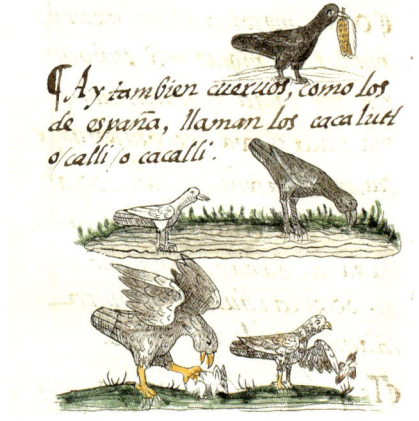

¶ Ay tambien cueruos, como los
de españa, llaman los cacalotl
o calli, o cacalli.

17. FAUNA

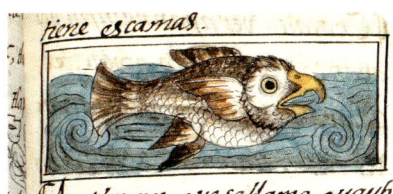

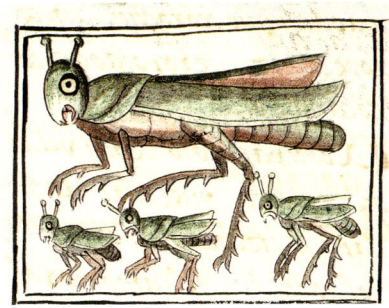

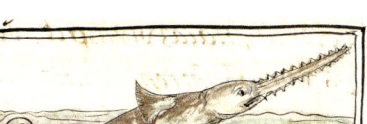

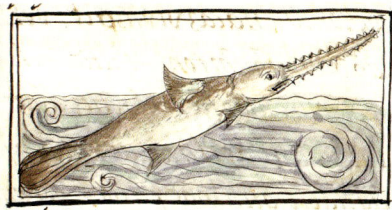

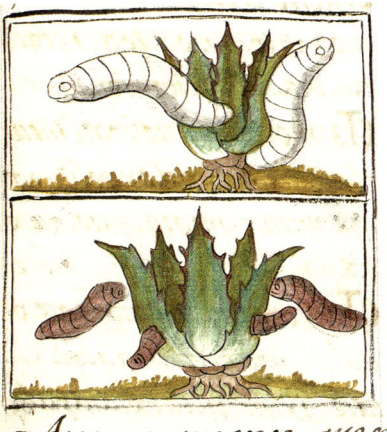

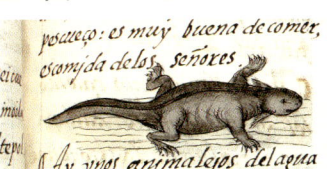

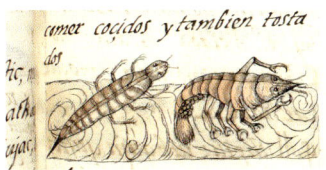

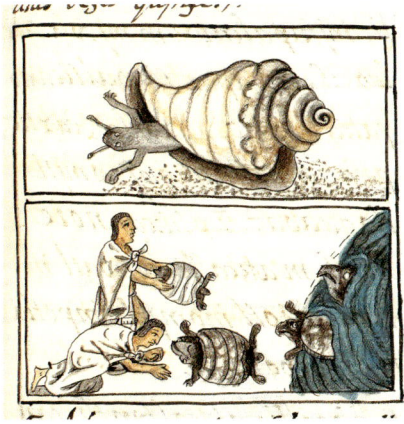

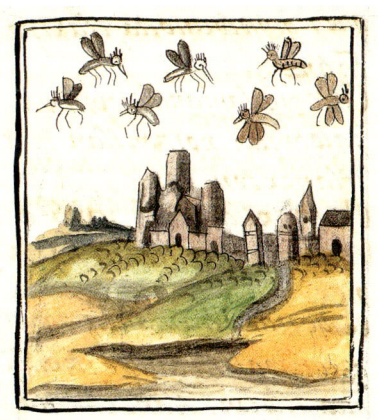

18. Smoking

Florence, Biblioteca Medicea Laurenziana, Med. Palat. 219, fol. 336r

In his description of the banquets held just before merchants departed on their travels, Sahagún writes: "As soon as they have finished eating, everyone washes their hands again and then each guest receives his own cup of cocoa, which they drink, and then the smoking tubes are handed round for sucking on". Reed smoking tubes, an early form of the pipe, were used for smoking tobacco and grasses, and were made as follows:

> The man who makes tubes for sucking smoke first of all cuts the reed and removes the leaves, cleaning it thoroughly. He grinds up the charcoal with which to line the reeds. Then he paints some and gilds others ... The painting work on some is hidden and only appears when they begin to burn ... There are lots of kinds of these tubes and they are filled with many different aromatic herbs, which are ground up and mixed together. They must be packed with rose petals, aromatic spices, bitumen, mushrooms ... and *iztzyetl*, which is a kind of grass ... And when they proffered the smoking tubes [opposite], they took the reed with their right hand, not at the uncovered end but the part covered with charcoal; and with the left hand they took the vessel on which the reed rested. The tube-server would say: "My lord, here is the tube of aromas", and the guest would take it up, place it between his fingers and begin to suck on it ... The tube was given and taken in the same way in which darts are thrown in battle. And the vessel stood for the shield, that is held in the left hand ... After this flowers were distributed...

In pre-Columbian Meso-America people smoked not only during banquets but also in religious ceremonies; besides pipes, which were filled with various herbs and grasses, they also smoked cigars made by rolling up tobacco leaves.

Another Meso-American habit was chewing gum, "the bitumen chewed by women, called *tzictli*". As Sahagún notes:

> Before it can be chewed they mix it with *axin* [a resin], to soften it ... And for the most part it is chewed by young adults, those who are already women; but not everyone chews it in public, just unmarried or young women, because the married women and widows do not do it in public but in their homes. The public women [prostitutes] shamelessly chew it anywhere, in the street, in the marketplace ... The reason why women chew *tzictli* is to ward off rheumatism and to dispel the bad odour of their mouths ... Men chew *tzictli* as well to prevent rheumatism and to clean their mouths, but do so in secret.

18. SMOKING

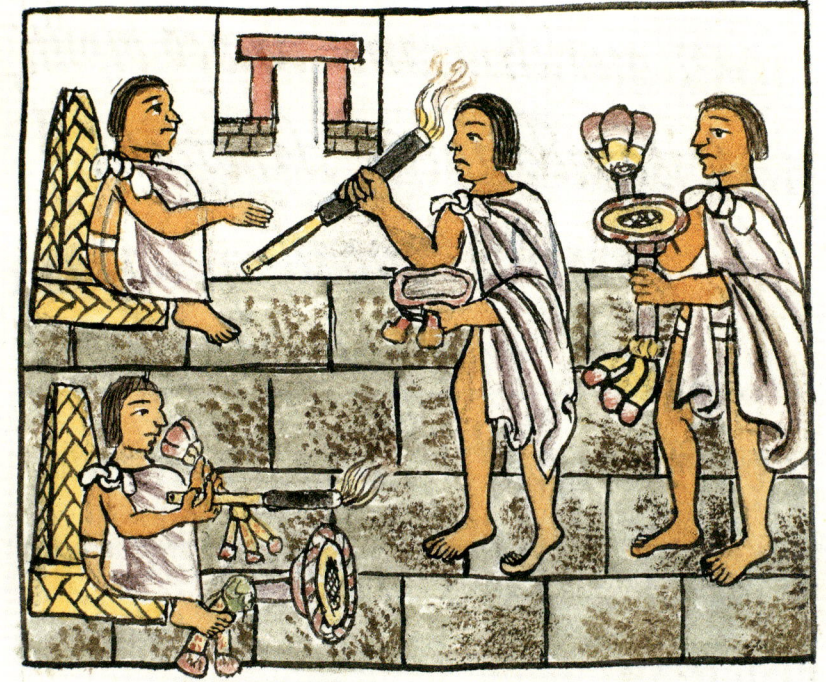

19. The arrival of Cortés

Florence, Biblioteca Medicea Laurenziana, Med. Palat. 220, fol. 406r

The twelfth and final book of the Florentine Codex deals with the Spanish conquest of Mexico, which took place between 1519, when Cortés landed on the Gulf Coast with just over one hundred men and a few horses, and 1521, when Tenochtitlán was taken and the Aztecs were definitively subjugated.

    Cortés headed for Mexico deliberately ignoring the orders of the governor of Cuba, Diego Velázquez, who had instructed him not to set sail and who made an attempt to thwart the exploits of the *conquistador* the following year by sending an expedition under the command of Pánfilo de Narváez. Cortés was so confident of success that a few days after landing he destroyed his ships so his men would not be tempted to return home or set out to conquer other lands. He pushed further and further inland, towards the Aztec kingdom, the most powerful in the region. Montezuma initially attempted a peaceful approach with the new arrivals, inviting them to leave and offering them, as Cortés himself reports in a letter to Charles V, generous gifts such as "pieces of gold, clothes and abundant provisions of hens, bread and cacao". This strategy was to no avail, however, and in 1519 the Spanish entered Tenochtitlán, first as 'friends' and then, when they took the king prisoner, as outright conquerors. They were forced to flee the city following a revolt, but on 13 August 1521 they re-entered the capital as victors.

    The key factors that determined the fall of the Aztec empire and victory for the Spanish were the ruthlessness of the soldiers, and of their commander in particular, who had no respect for the region's accepted codes of warfare; the use of firearms and horses, which the Meso-Americans had never previously seen; and above all Cortés's intuition that the peoples under the thrall of the Aztecs were prepared to join forces with him in order to shake off Aztec dominion.

19. THE ARRIVAL OF CORTÉS

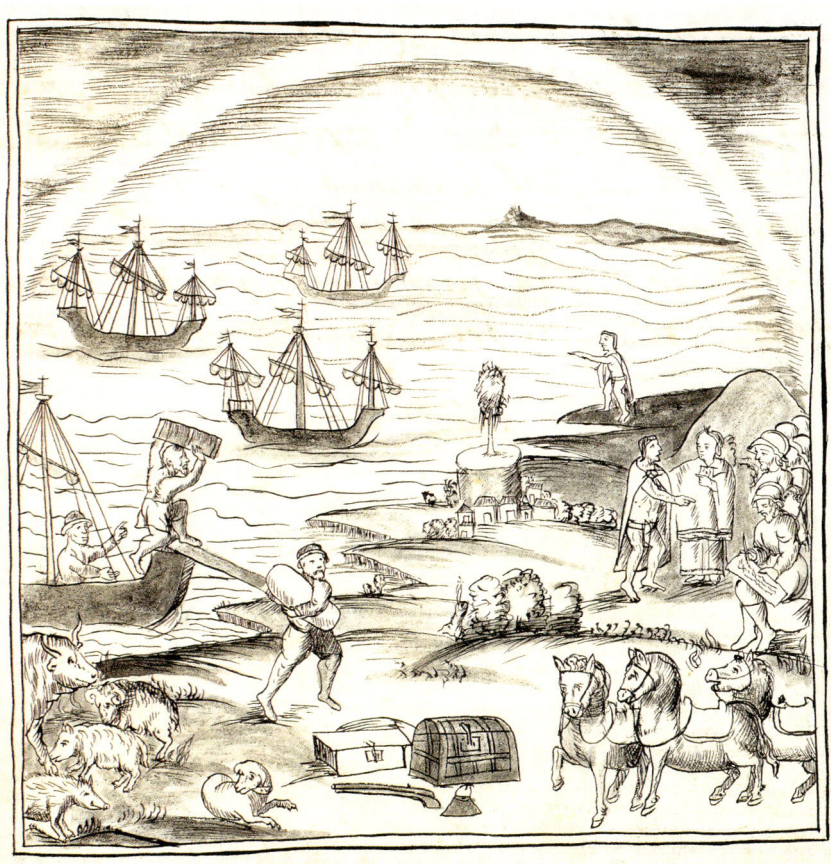

20. The Conquest

Florence, Biblioteca Medicea Laurenziana, Med. Palat. 220, fols. 454v, 461r, 476v, 460v

In his war of conquest Cortés received help from two figures in particular: Jerónimo de Aguilar, a Spaniard who had been shipwrecked on the Yucatán coast in 1517, was familiar with Mayan culture and could translate between Spanish and Maya; and particularly Doña Marina, also known as La Malinche (Malintzin), an indigenous noblewoman who had been reduced to slavery on the Gulf Coast, where a sovereign known as the Fat King offered her to Cortés soon after his arrival. Doña Marina spoke both Maya and Nahuatl, quickly picked up Spanish and acted as Cortés's interpreter, performing a fundamental role as an intermediary between the two cultures.

After Tenochtitlán, the Aztec capital, had been captured following a long siege, it was destroyed by the Spanish and rebuilt as the capital of New Spain. Sacred precincts and temples were burnt or razed to the ground, and the statues of the gods were destroyed, as were the Meso-American codices, the books that had preserved and handed down pre-Columbian religious thought and were of inestimable value. In the years following the conquest, churches and chapels were erected on the ruins of temples, and the population was forced to convert and be baptised, while human sacrifice was prohibited.

Decimated by wars and by unending exploitation on the part of the Spanish, the local population also had to deal with another unexpected affliction: the spread of diseases, probably typhoid fever and smallpox, that had been brought over by the Europeans and against which their immune systems had no defence.

20. THE CONQUEST

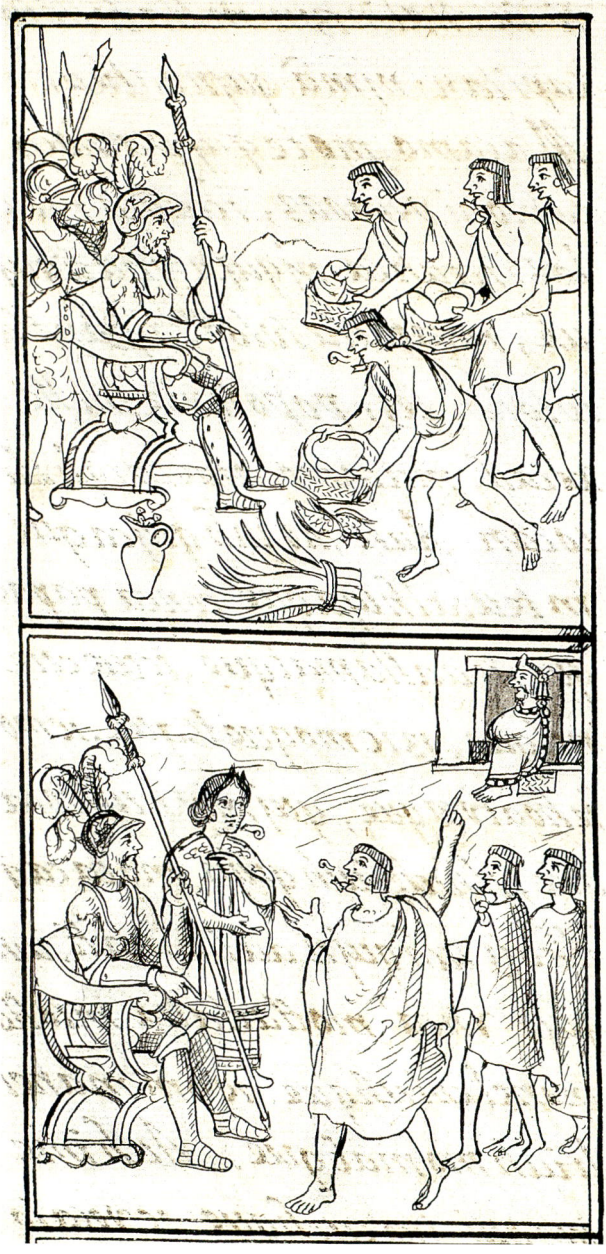

59

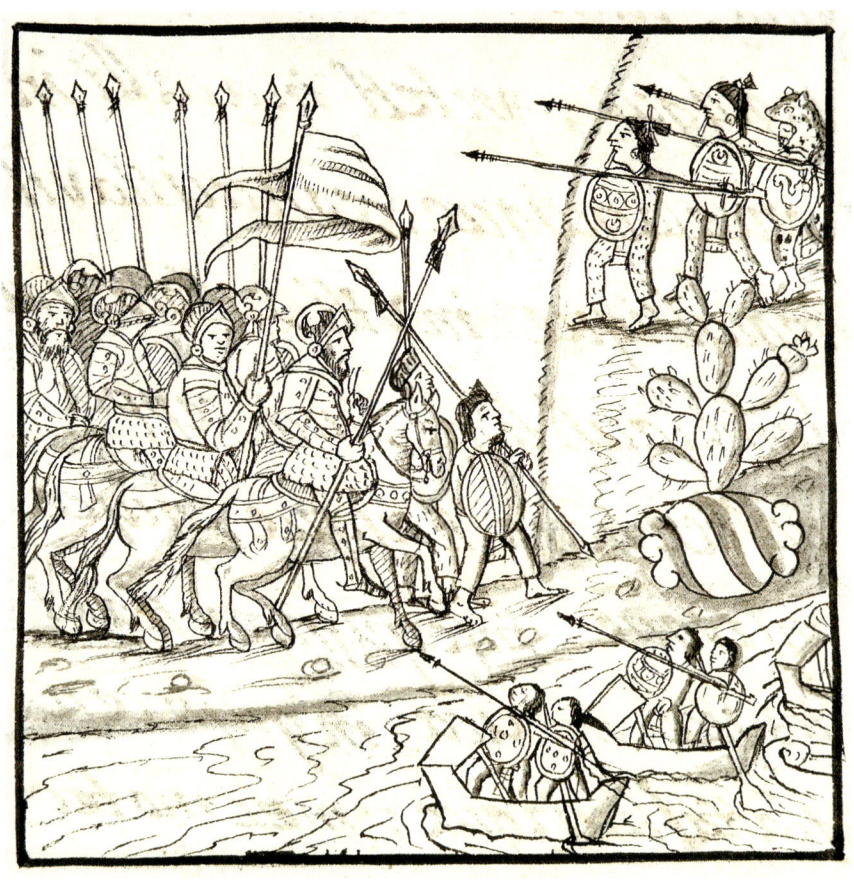

20. THE CONQUEST

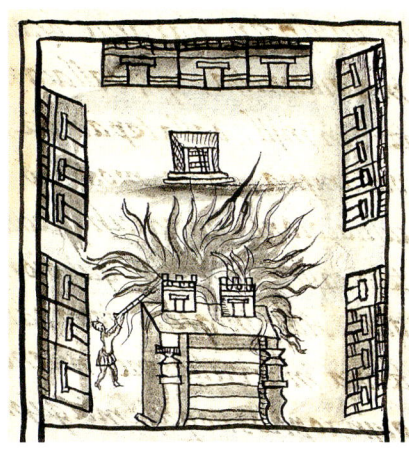

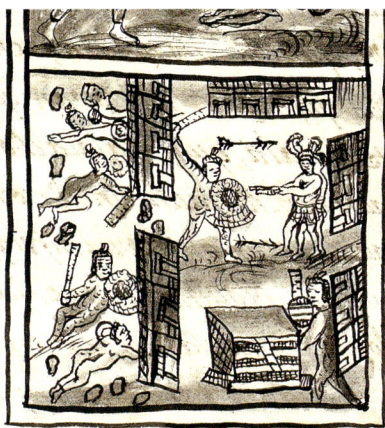

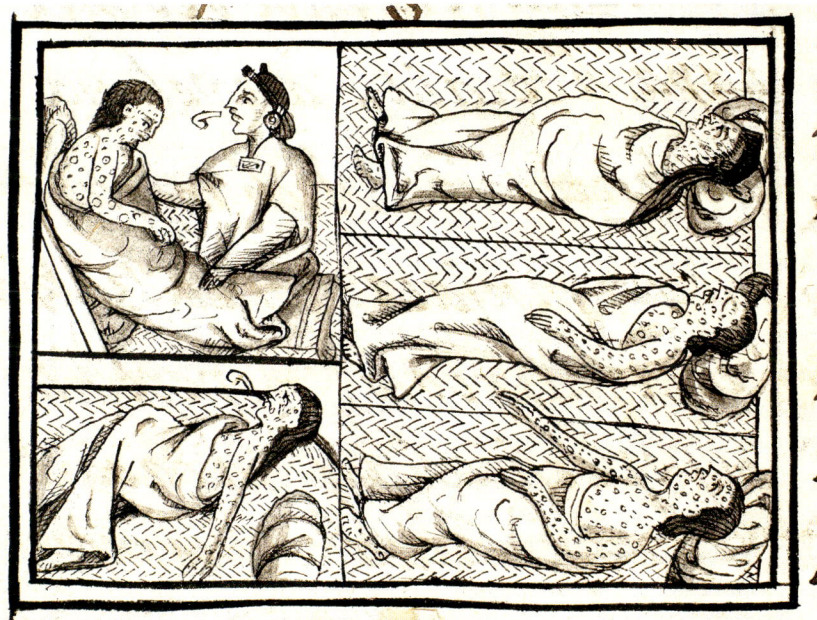

INDEX OF ILLUSTRATIONS FROM THE CODEX

Med. Palat. 218
  fol. 10r: 17
  fol. 52r: 47
  fol. 74rv: 29
  fol. 84v: 19
  fol. 100r: 11
  fol. 232v: 37
  fol. 250r: 32
  fol. 268r: 21
  fol. 275v: 37
  fol. 315r: 49
  fol. 329r: 33, 34–5

Med. Palat. 219
  fol. 228v: 31
  fol. 269r: 27
  fol. 280v: 41
  fol. 281v: 41
  fol. 292v: 27
  fol. 316r: 43
  fol. 336r: 55
  fol. 370r: 39

Med. Palat. 220
  fol. 26r: 40
  fol. 40r: 48
  fol. 71v: 45
  fol. 155v: 52
  fol. 173v: 52
  fol. 177rv: 52
  fol. 178r: 52
  fol. 198v: 52
  fol. 208v: 51
  fol. 209r: 51
  fol. 213v: 51
  fol. 215r: 53
  fol. 216r: 53
  fol. 217r: 52
  fol. 220r: 53
  fol. 222r: 53
  fol. 253v: 53
  fol. 256r: 53
  fol. 259v: 53
  fol. 406r: 57
  fol. 437v: 25
  fol. 454v: 59
  fol. 460v: 61
  fol. 461r: 60
  fol. 475r: 23
  fol. 476v: 61

TABLE OF CONTENTS

Preface	5
The Florentine Codex	7
Images from the Codex	
1. The gods	16
2. Sacrifice	18
3. Anthropophagy	20
4. The *tzompantli*	22
5. The Templo Mayor of Tenochtitlán	24
6. Games	26
7. Warriors	28
8. The rabbit in the Moon	30
9. The calendar	32
10. 'Baptism' and school	36
11. Feather art	38
12. The loom	40
13. Merchants	42
14. Cacao and chocolate	44
15. *Pulque*	46
16. Agriculture and food preparation	48
17. Fauna	50
18. Smoking	54
19. The arrival of Cortés	56
20. The Conquest	58
Index of illustrations from the Codex	62

Printed by Alpilito, Firenze
September 2007